The Home Counties
Edited by Mark Richardson

 Young**Writers**

First published in Great Britain in 2008 by:
Young Writers
Remus House
Coltsfoot Drive
Peterborough
PE2 9JX
Telephone: 01733 890066
Website: www.youngwriters.co.uk

SB ISBN 978-1 84431 504 8

Foreword

Young Writers was established in 1991 and has been passionately devoted to the promotion of reading and writing in children and young adults ever since. The quest continues today. Young Writers remains as committed to the nurturing of poetic and literary talent as ever.

This year's Young Writers competition has proven as vibrant and dynamic as ever and we are delighted to present a showcase of the best poetry from across the UK and in some cases overseas. Each poem has been selected from a wealth of *Little Laureates* entries before ultimately being published in this, our sixteenth primary school poetry series.

Once again, we have been supremely impressed by the overall quality of the entries we have received. The imagination, energy and creativity which has gone into each young writer's entry made choosing the poems a challenging and often difficult but ultimately hugely rewarding task - the general high standard of the work submitted ensured this opportunity to bring their poetry to a larger appreciative audience.

We sincerely hope you are pleased with this final collection and that you will enjoy *Little Laureates The Home Counites* for many years to come.

Contents

Courthouse Junior School, Maidenhead

James Dash (10)	14
Laura Howard (10)	15
Natalie Maine (11)	16
Georgia Wright (11)	17
Isobel Jobson (10)	18
Laura Paice (10)	18
Iona Collins (10)	19
James Hewitt (10)	19
Jade Guilloud-Stocke (10)	20
Alex Sloots (10)	20
James Carr (10)	21
Holly Bond (11)	21
Abigail Binning (10)	22
Hannah Fisher (11)	23
Anna Wheeler (10)	24
Katy Pocock (10)	24
Abhijeet Jandu (10)	25
Georgie Fahy (10)	25
Georgia Holgate (10)	26
Oliver Dew-Gosling (10)	26
Eleanor Duncombe (10)	27
Ben Walter (10)	27
Sarah Nugent (10)	28
Sam Lowe (10)	29
Lauren Bradley (10)	29
Emily Smith (10)	30
Ross Macrae (11)	30
Charlotte Bensch (10)	31
Henry Bowater (10)	31
Louie Fenwick (10)	32
Sam Lewis (10)	33

Datchet St Mary's CE Primary School, Slough

India Pyne (9)	33
Lettisha Roberts-Bent (9)	34
Tina-Marie Loveridge	34
Karanvir Singh (9)	34
Olivia Penfold-Campbell (9)	35
Chloe Randall-Barney (9)	35
Mariam Awan (9)	35

Molly Mason (10)   36
Anusha Stribbling (9)   36
Aaron Caldwell (9)   36
Samuel Nahar (9)   37
Sitara Duggal (9)   37
Rosie Beard (9)   37
Samuel Taylor (9)   38
Steven Mason (9)   38

Eagle House School, Sandhurst

Adam Bailey (10)   38
Liam Becker (9)   39
George Wilks (9)   39
Lily Rowlands & Menna Braithwaite (9)   39
Charlie Waters (9)   40
Ethan Bradd (9)   40
Amelia Golightly (9)   41
Robin Vonchek (9)   41
Rosie Saxby (9)   42
Catherine Allum (9)   42
Sophia Wallis (10)   43
Darcy Coop (9)   43
George Wallinger (10)   44
Daniel Cook (9) & Noah Walton (10)   44
Odise Vila & Richard Morgan (10)   45
Rudy Singh (9)   45
Nancy Kang   46
Charlie Riddell & Thor Winkler von Stioernhielm (10)   46
Yuna Kojima (11)   47
Ben Moore (9)   47
Laura Neat (9)   48
Tanaquille Manton-Jones & Ashley Inglis (9)   48
Mohammed Rubbani (9)   48
Ross Pawley-Kean (10)   49
Harry Baldock (9)   49
Adam Robinson (9)   49
Reece Williams (10)   50
Aanya Das & Maggie Knox (9)   50

Elham CE Primary School, Canterbury

Eleisha Lockwood (8)	50
Annie Gower (7)	51
William Herbert (8)	51
Alexandria Willoughby (7)	51
Tara Woodley (7)	52
Faris Cooke (8)	52
Isobel Van Eerten (7)	53
Ben Lewis (8)	53
James Lindsay (8)	54
Lily Theoff (7)	54
Ellie Pettit (8)	55
Fergus Dougal (8)	55
Charlotte Harbour (9)	56
Alex Hannah (8)	56
Emily Andrews (9)	57
Lauren-Amy Lord (7)	57
Lucy Barnes (9)	58
William Turnbull (9)	59
Jerra Wooding (10)	60
David Willoughby (8)	60
Sabrina Cook (8)	61
Eliza Gammon (10)	61
Eleanor Hart-Dyke (9)	62
Rosie Rutherford (9)	62
Max Wren (9)	63
Francesca Godden (8)	63
Megan Rutherford (9)	64
Sam Pratt (9)	64
Lotty Astbury (9)	65
Jacob Glass (9)	65
Elanah Harvey (9)	66

Highfield School, Maidenhead

Abigail Connor (10)	66
Alexandra Wilcox (10)	67
Elnaz Bedroud (10)	67
Eleanor Slade (10)	68
Maddie Merryweather (10)	69
Elsa Desmond (10)	69
Alice Lineham (10)	70

Catrin Williams (9)	70
Olivia Thomson (10)	71
Lily Streames-Smith (10)	71
Alexandra Kirkup-Lee (11)	72
Alice Armstrong (9)	73
Jaipreet Kaur Banwaith (8)	73
Sarah Williams (8)	74
Karina Law (9)	75
Paven Uppal (10)	75
Jodie Passmore (9)	76
Carmen Roca-Igual (9)	76
Tia Folley (9)	77
Natashia Berrio (8)	77
Annabel Chan (9)	78
Florence Weaver (9)	78
Georgina Lockwood (9)	79
Catherine Tren (9)	79
Rebecca Duffey (9)	80
Alice Slade (9)	80
Mollie O'Flaherty (9)	81
Elika Bedroud (9)	81
Sophie Bujakowski (8)	82
Kamini Khindria (9)	82
Sweta Pradeepkumar (8)	83
Ruby Griffiths (9)	83
Katie Parry (9)	84
Esme O'Sullivan (8)	85
Rebecca Clark (8)	86
Lucy Drew (9)	86
Rhianna Cross (8)	87

Kingsnorth CE Primary School, Ashford

Jamie Nichols (11)	87
Connor Robbins (10)	88
Daniel Holland (10)	88
Orla McGlone (10)	88
Hannah Terry (11)	89
Emma Croker (11)	89
William Ashdown (10)	89
Katie Wright (10)	90
Martin Nichols (11)	90

Melissa Garwood (10)	90
Tom Green, Jack Nutley & George Paul	91
Olivia Burt (11)	91
Sian Christopher (10)	91
Bradley King (10)	92
Josh Wright (11)	92
Kayleigh Winn (10)	93
Toby Morris (11)	93
Dan Bottachi (10)	93
Abigail Brown & Ashleigh Wheal (10)	94
Michael Payne (10)	94
Scott Roper (10)	95
Natasha Francis (11)	95
Callum Booth (10)	96
Jack Hardy (10)	96
Will Flockett (10)	96

Licensed Victuallers' Junior School, Ascot

Louise Rooker (10)	97
Devon Kivlehan (9)	97
Emily Howell (9)	97
Elizabeth Hamilton (10)	98
Tara Bharadia (9)	98
Zoë Carlin (10)	98
Rory Carmichael & Matthew Rawlinson (10)	99
Alanah Kendall (10)	99

Marish Primary School, Slough

Joseph Moore (10)	99
Chloe King El-Bokhari (11)	100
Scott Hensley (11)	100
Clare Highams (11)	100
Liam Condon (10)	101
Ellenna Brooks (11)	101
Daniel Blanchard (10)	101
Sohail Mir (11)	102
Liam Conlon-Highams (11)	102
Tevin Johnson (10)	102
Shai Bane (10)	103
Lucy Robbins (10)	103
Levi Stroud (10)	103

Vrinda Kanani (11)   104
Jordan Keeley (10)   104
Tilly Burden (11)   104
Qasim Durrani (10)   105
Rachel Hood (10)   105
Emma Hughes (10)   105
Hannah Nicholls (10)   106
Charles O'Neill (10)   106
Ghadiyah Mobashir (10)   106
Elliott Ogbebor (10)   107
Ryan Gulliford (11)   107
Shabazz Siddiq (10)   107
Srinithiy Aravinthanathan (10)   108
Charlie Hood (10)   108
Jasveet Heer (10)   109
Bradley Thorpe (10)   109

Moorlands Primary School, Reading
Tara Spargo (8)   109
Taylor Miles (8)   110
Gemma Driver (9)   110
Lekan Olasina (8)   110
Emma Harris (8)   111
Owen Gould (8)   111
Jack Chester (8)   111
Natasha Hallett (9)   112
Shannon Townley-Taylor (8)   112
Thomas Savin (8)   112
Charly Fox (8)   113
Chloe Clifford (8)   113
Amber Willis (8)   113
Ben Gowers (8)   114
Chloe Gunn (8)   114
Zoë Evans (8)   115
Molly Chandler (9)   115
Deven King (8)   116
Lydia Giles (9)   116
Dion Holley (8)   117
Gautham Senthilnathan (8)   117
Amy Thatcher (8)   118

Wildridings Primary School, Bracknell

The Poems

Mums And Children

M ums are the best in the world
U seful and happy
M ums are so beautiful
S o be grateful you have one to look after you

C hildren are fun and you should love them
H ow they love to run
I am happy I am one
L ying in my bed
D reaming happily
R eading my books
E veryone should like them
N early everybody does.

Chloe Howard (8)

Pirate Poems

There once was a pirate called Jack
Who wanted a gun in his back
He called out, 'Ahoy!'
And pulled at his toy
That silly old pirate called Jack.

There once was a pirate called Bill
Who wanted a bear called Will
But one stormy night he fell off his chair
With little care
That silly old pirate called Bill.

Opeluwa Ogundimu (10)

Why Can't I Have A Pet?

A dog, a cat, a fish, a hamster, a rabbit
Why can't I have a pet?
A Labrador as brown as chocolate
A poodle white as snow
A pug as grey as graphite in a pencil
A corgi, black as coal
A tortoiseshell kitten the colour of a turtle
A tabby that loves me
A ginger cat the colour of the sunshine
With eyes as blue as the sky
Red, yellow, orange and blue
Swimming in a tank -
Warm water fish and cold water fish
Why can't I have a pet?

Emily House (11)
Bradfield CE Primary School, Reading

Planet Of Dreams

A dream is a cute rabbit
Hopping on the floor
A dream is a haunted house
With a creaky door
A dream is an aerosol
With wet stuff inside
A dream is a huge lion
All filled with pride
A dream is a skyscraper
Small-looking from space
But my dream . . . is a . . .
Zzzzzzz.

Tommy Gaut (10)
Bradfield CE Primary School, Reading

Animals Rule The World

I feel asleep one frosty night
My dream went to the future
And it was set to the time
Where animals rule your life
Where everything was peaceful
As peaceful as a butterfly
Where animals could punish you
For anything you say.

The punishment was terrible
They make you grow their food
And if you get them angry
They are charging bulls
They catch you then they kill you
So I am glad it's just a dream.

Sarah Ellis (10)
Bradfield CE Primary School, Reading

Firebird

Firebird
As red as a rose
As elegant as a swan
As quick as a cheetah
As graceful as a cloud
As powerful as a ten ton elephant.

Firebird
As wise as a whale
As friendly as a puppy
A firebird would be a cool bird
What do you think?

Emma Meakin (10)
Bradfield CE Primary School, Reading

My Future

What shall I be when I grow up?
Maybe a jet pilot, rally driver, maybe an actor or a spy?

If I were a jet pilot, I would do stunts all day and never stop
Or show off to the farmer's crop and only stop for lunch
And write in the sky and twirl while I fly.

What about being a rally driver?
I could stung non-stop all day as I see the children play
Plus fill my trophy cupboard.

What about an actor?
I could become rich and fill the ditch
And famous with sports cars and super cars and a very big house.

Oh . . . what about being a spy?
I could have weapons and gadgets and secret bases
And go to lots of different places.

Which will I be?
I'll let time and destiny decide that for me.

Ross Maclean (10)
Bradfield CE Primary School, Reading

What Are Dreams?

Dreams are your own world
Dreams are a playground of thoughts
Dreams are a diary of life and death
Dreams are a stairway to a different land
Dreams are the place where your imagination lives
Dreams are the place you go when you go to sleep.

James Miller (11)
Bradfield CE Primary School, Reading

My Imaginary Friend

I snuggled up in my duvet as warm as could be
My eyelids were as heavy as boulders
I scrunched up as tight as a hamster
I fell asleep like a baby for the rest of the night.

In my dream I have a magic hand
Glowing so bright it would burn your eyes
My hand stretches to things in my room
Pulling things together to make a strange creature.

The head like a cuddly teddy bear
The arms like long cardboard tubes
The body like a bumpy plastic box
The legs like the smooth leg of a chair
Last but not least, the face like buttons.

Every night I get to see my imaginary friend
Again and again and again.

Amelia Richmond-Knight (10)
Bradfield CE Primary School, Reading

My Dream Job

What will I be when I'm older?
A footballer, a tennis player or coach?
As good as Stevie G
Or maybe be a failure?
I dream of what I will be
My dream job
Am I going to be famous?
Who knows?

Alex Bancroft (10) .
Bradfield CE Primary School, Reading

My Weird Dream

My eyes have closed
I am now in twilight
I had a dream, I'm not sure what
But I know for certain it wasn't good
It was *frightening, threatening, dangerous!*
Scary as death
I was walking home from school
Someone was watching me
It was *frightening, threatening, dangerous!*
I started walking faster
I heard voices in my head
They were *frightening, threatening, dangerous!*
I got home, went to bed
Fell asleep, woke up
And then realised
It wasn't a dream, *argh!*

Bethany Huff Guelbert (10)
Bradfield CE Primary School, Reading

Lunchtime

I dream of my crunchy salty crisps
And the chocolate bar that melts on my lips
I dream of my cold refreshing drink
All these thoughts of food make it hard to think.

I dream of sandwiches made of all these things:
Ham, Cheese, Tuna, Marmite, Chicken
And my apple as crunchy as snow
Which I save till last
I'm so excited
I just want the time to pass.

I check the clock to see the time
My tummy rumbles, I don't feel fine
Lunchtime means football and playtime too
I dream of lunchtime - why wouldn't you?

Ryan Rossington (11)
Bradfield CE Primary School, Reading

In My Dream

In my dream mospopoes suck their toe-toes
And the otters look like potters
When mospopoes do a dance the otters fall in a trance
Is this a nice dream?

In my dream kangareep with their manes as white as sheep
Stand by the water's edge, with their claws that cut down hedges
When the hedges call out stop, the kangareep hop off
Is this a nice dream?

In my dream twees are saviours when it comes to sheep
As they fight the baddies with their swordies
Whose antennae wave to me in the wind.

So don't you come to my dream with me
If you don't like: mospopoes who suck their toe-toes
Otters that look like potters
Kangareep who cut down hedges
And twees who are saviours for sheep.

Timothy Swinbank (10)
Bradfield CE Primary School, Reading

Magic Socks

Magic socks
Able to fit size 181 feet
They are super socks which were ordinary
But now are enchanted
As bright as the sun burning in summer
Soft as a cool cuddly cloud
Shiny, huge, mystical
Magic socks
Remind us of wizards and sorcery.

Alastair Borthwick (10)
Bradfield CE Primary School, Reading

Dreams

Dreams
Dreams are happy
Dreams are sad
Dreams are funny
Dreams are bad.

They are odd
They are whizzy
They are mad
They are busy
Dreams are mixed up, whisked up
Lots of things at once.

I wake up, sit up
The dreams have disappeared
Do you like dreams?
I hope you do
But I think I like them
More than you!

Holly Hutchings (10)
Bradfield CE Primary School, Reading

Frightful Nightmares

Frightful nightmares
They can scare the bravest man
Menacing, spooky, scary
As dreadful as a dragon
As terrifying as meeting the Devil
It makes me feel ghastly
It makes me feel like a baby
Frightful nightmares
They remind us our teachers aren't the scariest thing . . .

Ben Brown (10)
Bradfield CE Primary School, Reading

Lion

Mine is the growl
That fills with fright
In the dark mist
Mine is the night.

Mine are the dark eyes
That are full of fear
When I see danger
Mine is the ear.

Mine is the mane
That huntsmen steal
Mine is the mane
That is real.

Charlotte Appleton (9)
Cookham Rise Primary School, Maidenhead

Snake

Mine is the hiss that breaks the leaves
Mine is the eater in the zoo itself.

Mine is the fear that kills the pain
When danger is close, mine is the fear.

Mine is the scales
Mine is the eater
It is horrifying.

George Durrant (10)
Cookham Rise Primary School, Maidenhead

Jaguar

Mine is the growl that rocks the stones
In the forest bright, mine is the groan.

Mine is the nose that senses fear
When hunters near, mine is the ear.

Rhys Matthews (10)
Cookham Rise Primary School, Maidenhead

Dog

Mine is the bark
That chills the night
In the garden gloom
Awaiting the light.

Mine is the coat
All matted and unkempt
Sad and lonely
Nowhere to go.

Mine is the hunger
My food bowl is empty
All eaten and gone
Nowhere to go.

Aiden Back (9)
Cookham Rise Primary School, Maidenhead

Lion

Mine is the roar that fills the big top
With fear and doom
Hear my roar and feel your ears go pop.

Mine is the coat, the poacher's prey
I get tired at the end of the day
From running away from the poachers all day.

Joel Gormally (9)
Cookham Rise Primary School, Maidenhead

Bear

Mine is the growl that echoes around
Mine is the prowl that fills the ground.

Mine is the coat that belongs to me
Not huntsmen trade, I am afraid.

Jessica Lear (9)
Cookham Rise Primary School, Maidenhead

Dreams

In the silence of the night
When all the animals have gone to sleep
I hear a noise that gives me a fright.

My eyes are closed tight
My thoughts are racing
Why can I hear so many noises at night?

Slowly my eyes open
Everything is not as it seems
I realise it was only dreams.

Molly Savage (9)
Cookham Rise Primary School, Maidenhead

Gorilla

Mine is the roar that fills the big top
All day long, mine is the hop.

Mine is the pain that's chained to the floor
All day long, mine is the roar.

Mine is the flash that blinding flash
All day long, mine is the crash.

Max Woolfenden (10)
Cookham Rise Primary School, Maidenhead

Owl

Mine is the screech that fills the cage too small
Mine is the thud when I hit the wall.

Mine is the anger that boils up inside
Mine is the heart that longs to see outside.

Mine is the beak that teas up its prey
Mine are the wings that I soar on night and day.

Kate Lemon (9)
Cookham Rise Primary School, Maidenhead

Mine Is The Bite

Mine is the bite that wins a fight
Mine is the elite that even eats the prey's feet
Mine is the body that crushes all others
Mine is the body that was forced to consume my brothers.

Mine is the body as stretchy as a sling
Mine is the body that slithers under anything
Mine is the body that is no use now
Mine is the body that would rather die than eat a cow.

Mine is no use anymore
Mine is cold against the hard metal floor
Mine is the desolate and isolated body that you see before you
Mine is the withering body now no threat to you.

Luis Avellano-Khan (10)
Cookham Rise Primary School, Maidenhead

Crocs

Mine is the grunt, the killer of water
In the burning sun, mine is the fury.

Mine is the skin that's lost its scent
No longer strong, my body submerged.

Ben Isted (9)
Cookham Rise Primary School, Maidenhead

Sea Lion

Mine is the splash that gives people a bath
I do some tricks that makes them laugh.

Mine is the money they come to swim with my feet
I am very funny, mine is the treat!

Taylor Hartnett (9)
Cookham Rise Primary School, Maidenhead

Elephant

Mine is the trumpet that shakes the earth
In the empty night the elephant gave birth.

Mine is the skin that has lost its hair
No longer pregnant, stepped on a pin
And went through the skin.

Toby Palmer Godding (9)
Cookham Rise Primary School, Maidenhead

The Tall Man

Once there was a very, very tall man
Who woke up in an ice cream land
He took a very big bite
It did not taste right
He was chewing on his big fat pillow.

Christopher Tomling (10)
Cookham Rise Primary School, Maidenhead

Lion

Mine is the roar that scares everyone
But everyone realises it's only for fun.

Mine is the mane that is so shiny and gold
They make me exercise, but I am getting old.

Hamish Campbell (9)
Cookham Rise Primary School, Maidenhead

The Scythes Of Terror!

No feelings, no friends
Time for amends?
Not for the destruction that's been caused . . .

Cracked mountains
Burned cities
Ground covered
From fountains of fire . . .

Daggers strike over again
It spikes
It tears
How bad can it get . . .

People run, there's no escape
There he rumbles in the sky
Making it hard to survive . . .

Throwing his spears
Straight at the ground
Flashing towards the surface . . .

He runs, so fast
You can't even witness
Where his feet have passed . . .

Can you see him? Can you hear him?
You can feel him!
You'll feel where his feet have passed . . .

Too apathetic to show concern
Mindlessly slaughtering men
He is unstoppable
Hidden behind the clouds . . .

No feelings, no friends
Time for amends?
Not for the destruction that's been caused . . .

James Dash (10)
Courthouse Junior School, Maidenhead

The Bringer Of Morning

The Bringer of Morning,
Rises as I rise
Hurling out balls of flame into the ghostly sky
Stealing the night away.

She moves across the sky
Her ancient eye burning bright
Drifting across the grass
Making it shoot up healthily
Helping trees grow.

She can never die
Her eyes are kind and sparkling
And her ears can hear anything
Dancing through the blazing sky
Her footsteps leave no marks.

Suddenly the Bringer of Night appears
And a raging battle breaks out
The Bringer of Morning tries her best
But the Bringer of Night
Tries harder.

The Bringer of Morning fails to win
And the Bringer of Night forces her to her cage
She spends the night burning the bars
And by morning she escapes.

The Bringer of Morning,
Rises as I rise
Hurling out balls of flame into the ghostly sky
Stealing the night away.

Laura Howard (10)
Courthouse Junior School, Maidenhead

The Witch Of The Moon

The sunset is over and the Witch of the Moon
Dances, laughing, over the darkest hills
Spreading silver, neither liquid nor gas
At the lightest touch of her slippers.

Her robe of white trails far behind
Adding sparkles to the dullish gloom
As the bats that usually shadow the Earth
Fly, entranced, to form a crown

Round her head, which dances and twirls
As she swoops down low over twilight houses
Handing nightmares to the bad
And sweet dreams to the good.

But when the tip of the sun begins to show
The bats fly away and the dreams are gone;
And the Witch of the Moon sweeps up her carpet
Of silver and sparkles with a touch of gold.

As the sun creeps up, higher and higher
She swoops up high to reach the moon
Where she sleeps in shadow until Day grows weak
And she can start the night cycle once more.

Natalie Maine (11)
Courthouse Junior School, Maidenhead

The Siblings Of The Sky

The Golden Jester skips through the fields
He becomes lovely when a smile he wields
The Princess of Stars stares deep in the mirror:
Her heart grows colder as her soul shrinks thinner
He never seeks but will always find
A plain-faced child with a beautiful mind
Cold and graceful, yet all alone -
Not an inch of kindness has she ever been shown
The sun shines down on his friendly face
About his head bright butterflies chase
Beautiful on the outside, beastly within -
She has no lover, friends or kin
The breeze joins him in play and his sandy hair flies
Temporarily blinding sky-blue eyes
Eternally brushing chocolate hair;
Hatred consumes her - it poisons the air
Cheerful and miserable
A laugh and a cry;
Characteristically contrary
Are the siblings of the sky.

Georgia Wright (11)
Courthouse Junior School, Maidenhead

Global Warming

The ice caps are melting from all the pollution
Polar bears are nearly extinct
Waves are sweeping over islands
To sort out the problems we must try to think.

Save the world from all these things!

Has anyone thought of the future?
Their children, how will they live?
Millions of people all dying of hunger
And what if there's no food to give?

Save the world from all these things!

Unpredictable weather has started
Seasons are changing too soon
Data's downloaded
The results are now charted, so . . .

Save the world from all these things.

Isobel Jobson (10)
Courthouse Junior School, Maidenhead

Released

It has swallowed all the air
It's now set free
Clothed in a glossy red, clashing with the sky
Up among the trees, taken by the wind
Hoping not to get killed by the spiny branches.

Heading for the sun with his string following him
Alone, but feeling good
Bouncing and jumping in the morning mist
Hiding in the clouds
Resting on a fluffy mattress.

Laura Paice (10)
Courthouse Junior School, Maidenhead

The Dreams Of The Night

The Delicate Princess flies through the night
Caring for others whilst they sleep
But the only thing that makes her unhappy
Is watching her sister make them weep.

The Evil Torturer flies through the night
Scouring the skies for sleep
But the only thing that makes her happy
Is watching the children wake up and weep.

The Delicate Princess flies through her castle
Wondering when her sister will see reason
Stroking her pet, she says out loud,
'Why did my sister do treason?'

The Evil Torturer flies through the castle
Wondering why her mother sees reason
In her little sister and then chanted,
That her mother banished her for treason!

Iona Collins (10)
Courthouse Junior School, Maidenhead

The Lord Of Darkness

Daring myself to pass the Lord of Darkness
With my blood rushing up to my head
A scary nasty burglar
The Lord of Darkness was molten lava.

Red fiery eyes stared down at my tracks
Black smoking breath attacking me
He shouted at my soul and shot at my thoughts
I've met the Lord of Darkness and Death!

James Hewitt (10)
Courthouse Junior School, Maidenhead

Wars Go On Forever

Wars go on forever
Causing poverty and homes to explode
People always die and never live
Like they have no other choice
Bombs explode overhead
And shake the entire town
Every day, somewhere, a building crashes down
People see no sense
In shaking hands in agreement
Because they think fighting is
The only way of achievement
To fight and start killing
Is not the only way of winning
Wars go on forever
Causing poverty and homes to explode
People always die and never live
Like they have no other choice
Bombs explode overhead
And shake the entire town
Every day, somewhere, a building goes down.

Jade Guilloud-Stocke (10)
Courthouse Junior School, Maidenhead

The Strong Slave

The mindless slave, great and tall,
Lifts up pipes, glinting and shining.
His big heavy eyes stare as he moves
The lonely creature dressed in chains
Obeys his master and makes things change
Clanging and banging, turning his arm
He groans and shifts, looking down at the world
As he moves he creaks and shudders making things new.

Alex Sloots (10)
Courthouse Junior School, Maidenhead

The Shining Protector

I met in a wood one day
A beautiful golden goddess
With shining yellow eyes
And a radiant robe of neatherweave
That flows through blinding light.

The animals stand in her midst
She alights gently on their shoulders
Pats them and strokes them
A mother nursing a cub.

But suddenly the hunters come
A switch is thrown
And quick as a whip the protector
Rises up and vanquishes its foe
The morning light destroying darkness.

I met in a wood one day
A shining protector
Lethal, but gentle
Deadly, but sweet.

James Carr (10)
Courthouse Junior School, Maidenhead

Ruler Of Gloom

Wandering miserably through the streets
Wonder what he would meet
Pattering through the lonely village
Clashing and trashing, past the baker's and the butcher's
No one dared to go and greet him
Thundering down to the forgotten forest
Then he stopped . . . dead in his tracks
And disappeared to the middle of nowhere.

Holly Bond (11)
Courthouse Junior School, Maidenhead

School

Why do we say, 'Down with school, I hate school,'
When really it is quite fun
Every day we walk, run and play in a playground
Friendly and kind.

School's not so bad
You *can* get your dream job
If you have an education
That is what school is about.

We can go to university
Unlike some poor souls in Africa or Iraq
They need money and without money . . .
No school.

Africans, Iraqis or Afghans
Want school so much
But we just sit there thinking
Wish we were at home.

They can't get jobs
They can't do anything
Without an education
But . . .

We still sit there thinking,
Why school, why?
Really we shouldn't
Because school's *cool!*

Abigail Binning (10)
Courthouse Junior School, Maidenhead

Child Of The Wild

All is quiet by the lake
Until the child of the wild grows
A dress of white, with colourful flowers
A rosy-red face full of smiles
Eyes alight with blue, glinting in the sun
Hair all blonde with glossy brown streaks
Making everyone around feel comforted and safe
She jumps and runs with joy
Dragging you into a world of wildness.

Her dress is now a reddy-yellow
With tints of orange here and there
The rosy-red face now looking tired
The smiles are nearly all gone
Her eyes now look dim
Rather than a light blue
Her hair is now quite straggly, from all the wind and rain
She makes people around feel less cheerful
As the colours start to fade
Taking you away from the wildness
She drops into slumber.

Hannah Fisher (11)
Courthouse Junior School, Maidenhead

Stormy Season

Marching soldiers
And the boom of a drum
Down the rivers, here we come
The strike of a sword
And a clash of a chord
Down to the river waters.

Here they come
Onto the sky
Way up in the mountain high
With its best friend breeze
It swings through the trees
Down the river waters.

There they go in rippling waves
But they'll be back
In future days.

Anna Wheeler (10)
Courthouse Junior School, Maidenhead

Danny Sundae

Danny Sundae lives on a hill
He parts the clouds
And spreads light where he walks
He laughs and jokes with his best friend, Heat
His blond spiky hair
Gives joy to all he meets
But when the night comes
Everyone gets into bed
So he packs up his bags
To give glee somewhere else
So when you wake up
Look out of the window and say,
'Good morning Mr Sundae, come out and play!'
Hey, Mr Sundae come out today!

Katy Pocock (10)
Courthouse Junior School, Maidenhead

Horror Of The Night

A dull suit of black and brown
A face full of guilt
A smile of pure evil
And eyes of massive destruction.

Going through the dusty town
Round the corners of the street
Destroying everything in its path
There's nowhere to hide from this devastating demon.

A rolling ball of flame
Like a heart, it goes on non-stop
Burning everything into ash
Painful damage to the town.

Like a developing child with every crisp of ash
It grows bigger every second
Once its time is up, it rests until . . .
The moment comes, for it to start again.

Abhijeet Jandu (10)
Courthouse Junior School, Maidenhead

The Breeze Blower

He jumps and leaps
Swivels and swerves
Steals and scars
He's cold and bitter
Those bright blue eyes
His scruffy hair
He won't leave you alone
He's always there
He'll tease and torture
And late at night when you're asleep
He'll sneak through your window without a sound
In a flash he will go
Flying to a place that no one else knows.

Georgie Fahy (10)
Courthouse Junior School, Maidenhead

The Golden Goddess

Skipping, singing
As she passes
Giving us joy
And light every day.

Her house drifts upon
White feathery clouds
Whilst the lady of sunlight
Prances happily in the silver sky.

Her long blonde curls
Plaited in ribbons of golden sunlight
Rest on an orange and yellow silk dress
Embroidered with sunflower petals.

I look up to her
Every day at sunrise
Wondering of what joy
She will give us for the day ahead.

Georgia Holgate (10)
Courthouse Junior School, Maidenhead

The Sea Stalker

Sweeping slowly across the ocean floor
He kicks his back legs furiously
Round and round
His black, streamlined shape
Glides through the sea
Slowly two long arms extend from his body
A sight, with a resemblance to a gun's
Breaks the surface of the water
He is going to attack . . .
His one eye finds the target . . .
And the arms break free of his body at speed.

Oliver Dew-Gosling (10)
Courthouse Junior School, Maidenhead

Twinkling Alone

I stand all alone
In the black inky sky
My light shining brightly
Glistening like a dazzling diamond.

I feel sad and melancholy
Searching desperately for a companion
Oh how I would love a friend
To dance, sing and play with.

My wise old friend, Lunar
Comforts and assures me
His strength so powerful
Like a parent - he consoles me.

I stay ever hopeful
That a friend I will find
To end this lonesome existence
I seek to love, for with it I will keep on shining
Forever.

Eleanor Duncombe (10)
Courthouse Junior School, Maidenhead

The Shining God

Walking down the dark dull alley
He shone and made an enormous light
His glistening body, all yellow and orange
Sparkling colours on his gown
Shining with his bright clothes
Moving slowly to and fro
His eyes glittering in the morning
Looking out for further glory
There he was lighting the alley
He shone and made an enormous light.

Ben Walter (10)
Courthouse Junior School, Maidenhead

The Storyteller

There are many storytellers
Though I met the overseer
Her face was pale
She had no eyes
No ears either side
But a mouth and tongue
Made for telling stories.
She had a cloak of words, which draped on the floor
Making it look as if she had no legs
Her hair was ice, tied together with fire
Making her look scary and very kind at the same time.

They move slowly, slowly and silently
Crawling from the bookshelf
Out, into the light of your bedroom
Ready to speak words of wisdom
Their tales would go on forever
Making you laugh or cry until you know you will have to stop.

There are many storytellers
Though I met an overseer
She took me into an action-packed world and a mysterious land
Where there was everything imaginable
I love storytellers
Especially the one I met last night.

Sarah Nugent (10)
Courthouse Junior School, Maidenhead

Brown Bear

We hunt you, Brown Bear
For your soft brown fur.

Unlucky Brown Bear
Too bad, don't care.

Your fur makes us clothes and things
Your meat is delicious for our dinner to come.

Unlucky Brown Bear
Too bad, don't care.

Your heads are trophies, ornaments
We keep your legs for stylish dress.

Unlucky Brown Bear
Too bad, don't care.

Soon there's only one of you
Oh dear, what did we do?

Oh dear Brown Bear
Oh dear, we care.

Sam Lowe (10)
Courthouse Junior School, Maidenhead

Shadow Of Darkness

She drifts scarcely in and out of the shadows
Treading with bare feet on soft damp grass
Her jet-black hair whisks around in the powerful wind
As the butterflies flutter about the thistle
Which looms over her head
Her midnight-blue eyes glisten as she looks up
At the full moon that shines above.
As she moves, she makes no sound
Only the call of the owl is heard.

Lauren Bradley (10)
Courthouse Junior School, Maidenhead

Aquatic Fury

A shimmer of blue, I saw as I fell
A cheerful giggle, I heard as well.

Her face, cheerful and bright and cheeky too
Golden ribbons dangled from her blonde hair
Ocean-green pearls for eyes.

Silver sparkled from her arms and legs
The dolphins called something,
Something I missed.

The waters started to rage
Sea creatures fled
Currents strengthened
I cried out, although it was useless down there.

Her face was now burning and furious
She stood statue-still as the waters attacked.

A shimmer of blue, I saw as I awoke
A cheerful giggle, I heard once again.

Emily Smith (10)
Courthouse Junior School, Maidenhead

In the Valley

Running through the valley on feet as soft as light
Hair twisting and turning, lapping at her face
Twinkling stars reflected in her slushing gown
Gushing around her body
On stormy nights her anger froths
Rocks shrinking under her angry glare
Tree trunks, leaves and flowers float on her dress of midnight-blue.

And in the morning, while all is resting
She's swishing and swirling amiably
As if nothing has happened
Finally, her journey over, the Water Maiden
Reaches the deep beauty of her salty home.

Ross Macrae (11)
Courthouse Junior School, Maidenhead

Daughter Of Fire

A world so dark
A light so bright
She dances and twirls
To ease the night.

Her glistening sheet
Of golden hair
Her emerald-green eyes
Are there to stare.

Her big black belt
Her long red dress
Her luminous shoes
She dressed to impress.

With her kind caring nature
Why is she so lonely?
Her glowing personality
She shines so bravely.

Charlotte Bensch (10)
Courthouse Junior School, Maidenhead

The Smashing Crawler

This smashing beast, that crawls over the ground
Rips up soil whilst wailing with pain
His eyes flash on gates and walls
He groans so loudly that the earth shakes
He eyes the next bit of ground and slowly moves to attack
Digging his shovels into the grass
He pulls, he lifts, throws and collects
He lives in a shed, all shabby and grey
But there is not time to rest as his commander shouts orders
His next piece of work involves so much more pain
He groans and moans, shudders and shakes
But he finishes and stands up tall, proud of his work
Now it's all dark and he crawls to his shed
Rest for the whole weekend ahead.

Henry Bowater (10)
Courthouse Junior School, Maidenhead

The Flaming Torch

The Flaming Torch
Flying through the black sky
Above the misty clouds
Lighting up the world with his anger
His golden flaming hair
Catching the eye from a mile away
People amazed by his silky red cloak burning strong.

If you touch his angry body
You will be hurt by his impossible strength
He is looking ahead, waiting for it to appear
And then there is a light in the distance.

Can it be?
It is! It is!
It is his home
He flies full pelt
Towards the dazzling ball of flame
And then, he is gone.

Louie Fenwick (10)
Courthouse Junior School, Maidenhead

Climate Change

Ice caps are melting
Water becomes poison
It doesn't mean hot holidays
With animals being killed.

The atmosphere is splitting
Carbon dioxide is overwhelming
There aren't any more planets
Without poisoned atmospheres.

Do something about it
It's all up to you
We were given this planet to enjoy
Not to destroy.

Lots of evil factories
Blowing out CO_2
Quickly, stop it happening
Before it's too late!

Sam Lewis (10)
Courthouse Junior School, Maidenhead

Colours

Black is like the deep black fur of the rat
Yellow is the colour of the golden Syrian hamster's fur
Silver is the colour of necklaces and chains glimmering in
the moonlight
Brown is the colour of a delicious sparkling glass of Coke
Orange is the colour of juicy tangerines.

India Pyne (9)
Datchet St Mary's CE Primary School, Slough

Colours

Orange is the colour of evening sun, setting in the west
Red is a sparkling shining ruby as dark as blood
Yellow is the summer's dazzling light
Grey is the colour of autumn's torrential showers
Black is a silk sheet in the midnight sky
White is the colour of a swan's waterproof feathers
Green is the long grass.

Lettisha Roberts-Bent (9)
Datchet St Mary's CE Primary School, Slough

My Poem Of Colour

Pink is the colour of flowers blowing in the wind
Red is juicy, tasty cherries from branches on the tree
Blue is the colour of the waves out at sea
Black is the night sky without sparkling stars
Yellow is a ball of golden fire in the sky.

Tina-Marie Loveridge
Datchet St Mary's CE Primary School, Slough

Colours Of The World Forever

Black is as dark as a plimsoll on my foot
Red is an evil lady's blood
Green is like an emerald-green leaf swishing about
Blue is sea waves crashing on the shore
Grey is like a silver medal swinging around the man's neck.

Karanvir Singh (9)
Datchet St Mary's CE Primary School, Slough

Colours Of The Rainbow

Green is like the leaves that sprout out in spring
Yellow is like the shining sun in the middle of the day
Blue is like the river flowing slowly through the land
Pink is the cheeks of a very smiley person who is very happy
Red is the colour of blood and a sign of evil
Black is the colour of bats that are flying in a haunted house.

Olivia Penfold-Campbell (9)
Datchet St Mary's CE Primary School, Slough

Colours Of The Rainbow

Red is a sweet-smelling rose
Black is the dark Devil's heart
Purple is like the Queen's royal crown and cloak
Blue is sapphire-blue crystal
Pink is the colour of Piglet's curly tail.

Chloe Randall-Barney (9)
Datchet St Mary's CE Primary School, Slough

Colours

Red is as bright as a shiny ruby glowing on my ring
Gold is the jewellery just fit for a king
Green is like the bushes swaying in the breeze
White is a handkerchief just for when I sneeze
Yellow is the sun shining everywhere
Blue is the uniform that I wear.

Mariam Awan (9)
Datchet St Mary's CE Primary School, Slough

Colours

Black is as dark as shiny shoes after you've bought them
Yellow is the sun that keeps us warm all through the day
Blue is the sea that throws waves at everything near it
Green is like grass that grows and animals eat
Red is as hot as fire burning a house down or roaring in a bonfire.

Molly Mason (10)
Datchet St Mary's CE Primary School, Slough

Colours Of Faces And The World

Black is a witch's pot cooking under the night sky
White is an egg beginning to fry
Blue is like Anthony crying his eyes out
Red is the colour of my brother's face when he lies
Purple is the colour of my grandpa's face
When he found out that his dad died.

Anusha Stribbling (9)
Datchet St Mary's CE Primary School, Slough

Colours, Colours

Red is the colour of blood bleeding from my leg
Black is the colour of the shadow lurking around
Yellow is like the sun gazing down at us from the sky
Blue is the sea roaring, rumbling and crashing boats about
Silver is the colour of a shiny knight's armour in the moonlight.

Aaron Caldwell (9)
Datchet St Mary's CE Primary School, Slough

Colours

Black is as dark as the silent night
Blue is the deep blue sea
Green is like the swaying grass
Gold is shiny pound coins in my hand
Yellow is like bright shiny sand at the beach.

Samuel Nahar (9)
Datchet St Mary's CE Primary School, Slough

Colours Of The World

Brown is the colour of my beautiful skin
Blue is like the deep blue sea where dangerous creatures live
Green is the colour of sparkling emeralds
Yellow is the colour of the sun sparkling in the sky
Purple is the colour of royalty.

Sitara Duggal (9)
Datchet St Mary's CE Primary School, Slough

Poem Of Colours

Red is shimmering rubies shining like glossy lips
Yellow is daffodils swaying in the fresh wind
Gold is the sun glowing through the summer's day
Green is the grass swaying in the breeze
Blue is a swimming pool where children splash about.

Rosie Beard (9)
Datchet St Mary's CE Primary School, Slough

The Spectrum And Beyond

Blue is the beautiful, clear, summer sky
Red is like a wild angry fire burning bright
Green is as shiny as the precious emerald
Yellow is as bright and cheerful as a field of daffodils
Black is as dark as the evil cloak we call the night.

Samuel Taylor (9)
Datchet St Mary's CE Primary School, Slough

Super Colours

Blue is the sea crashing into rocks
Yellow is like the sun shining down on us
Red is like the lava sizzling, ready to burst
Green is the grass swishing in the wind
Orange is like the sun setting over the sea.

Steven Mason (9)
Datchet St Mary's CE Primary School, Slough

Apples

I love apples they give me the heebie geebies
The way I bite into the strong hard skin
Into the cold watery inside
And move into hard outline of the pips
The green apples, the red apples
Russet, the violet and the yellow
I like to hide one under my pillow.

Adam Bailey (10)
Eagle House School, Sandhurst

In The Garden

I run around my garden
I sprint to my sandpit
Then tiptoe to the Wendy house
Open the door and cheerfully have a club meeting
Then I walk to the trampoline and do a trick
My mum calls me in, I hop to her
I love my mum and I'll always keep my love with her
And at night she gives me a hug and tucks me in tight.

Liam Becker (9)
Eagle House School, Sandhurst

Winter

Frosty, gleaming, glittering, white snow
Freezing, terrific, hard ice
Frost caves, glittering ice crystals
Snow mountains full with white snow
I can hear the children cheering and chanting
'Watch out, snowball!'

George Wilks (9)
Eagle House School, Sandhurst

Parrot

His outspread wings are a magnificent rainbow
He soars over the rich green canopy
Swooping down, tearing open juicy jungle fruits
Weaving in and out of the beautiful high trees.

Lily Rowlands & Menna Braithwaite (9)
Eagle House School, Sandhurst

Travelling Around The World

Walking through the busy streets
Skiing down the mountain pistes
Strolling across the boating jetty
Sailing the river, cold and windy
Travelling across the dusty plains
Seeing the animals roaring and lazing in the shade
Hacking through the dense jungles
Crawling through the dark tunnels
Looking up at the towering trees
Seeing the monkeys upon the trees
Though travelling the world is lovely
It's nice to be at home watching telly.

Charlie Waters (9)
Eagle House School, Sandhurst

The Trilobite

An armoured flatworm
With an in-built shield
In front of its sandpaper eyes
Brown or black
So is the skin
Over sixty railway lines
Sprouting from the main station
Split into terminals for each pair.

Ethan Bradd (9)
Eagle House School, Sandhurst

My Old Tree

My old tree standing there quite still
When autumn is here
She starts to cry, falling leaves
Orange and brown from her beautiful face
All the leaves are dead on the ground
Months go by so quickly
Spring reaches my garden
My old tree has her luscious leaves back
She's so happy,
Bright green leaves no longer on the ground.

Amelia Golightly (9)
Eagle House School, Sandhurst

The Komodo Dragon

It crawls in silence
A venomous horror
Snatching life
Its claws tearing through the earth
At times up trees
At times in the water
Its teeth daggers
Its skin as rough as a tree's bark
Its tongue a snake ready to strike.

Robin Vonchek (9)
Eagle House School, Sandhurst

My Favourite Tree

My favourite tree is a gnarled old tree
With rosy-red apples, all ripened for me
With shady branches where I like to read
Where I lie on my back watching fluffy clouds spread
My favourite tree is a special ancient tree
As it has been there for years and years
Surviving through weather, fierce or calm
It never seems to show any fears
I like my precious old tree
She will always be here for me.

Rosie Saxby (9)
Eagle House School, Sandhurst

Girls In Our Class

I am called Clever Kitty, people call me clever
My best friend is diva queen Darcy, she's a real diva queen
Bouncing Beth is the best at bouncing
Smart Sophia keeps her head in a book
Tall Tink is so tall, she's the tallest
Leaping Laura leaps from stone to stone
Marvellous Milly is great at making cakes
That's the girls in my class
Wacky, weird and wonderful.

Catherine Allum (9)
Eagle House School, Sandhurst

Playtime

Fantastic four square
Wilderness woods
What shall I do?
Smashing swimming
Nerve-racking netball
I haven't got a clue!
Terrific trampolining
Crazy cross-country
I haven't got time to choose
The wilderness woods
I'll choose that today
Now I really feel
I'm ready to play.

Sophia Wallis (10)
Eagle House School, Sandhurst

Spring

Spring is my favourite season
Because it's when I dance,
I dance around my gorgeous garden
And boy, I'm very fast
The pretty flowers grow
And I wear a bow
One thing I have to say
it's very cheerful
It's very good
Because spring is on its way
I go outside and pick the green grass
I make daisy chains too!

Darcy Coop (9)
Eagle House School, Sandhurst

Anne Frank

Sitting in my corner
Looking at the birds outside
Bored, lonely, tired, afraid
Wondering -
How will this stop?
When will this stop?
Hearing the sirens outside
And the screaming of people being taken away
Torn apart from their families.

I want to escape
To run in the wind
And feel the air sting my face
Brush my hands and legs on the snow
I want to talk to my friends
Eat ice cream in the summer
And slurp hot chocolate in the winter
I want to be free to make a noise
Hula hoop and swim
I need to believe this will happen.

George Wallinger (10)
Eagle House School, Sandhurst

The Worm

Pink and slimy
Like a newborn baby
A plaster at the end of its squiggly body
Like a cut finger
Slithering and wiggling
To its underground home.

Daniel Cook (9) & Noah Walton (10)
Eagle House School, Sandhurst

The Secret Annexe

Tiptoeing every day on the creaky floor
Missing the nature
The fresh air
Missing the sunlight.

In these old damp rooms
Hearing gunshots
Imagining horrors
Hiding from the enemy
Hearing bombs exploding
Living terror.

I want to be outside
To play with my friends
Swim in the sea like a fish
Run through the fields like a deer
I hope the war will end soon
And I will fly free like a bird.

Odise Vila & Richard Morgan (10)
Eagle House School, Sandhurst

If Only

If only I had a bed to sleep in at night.
If only I had a mum and dad to tuck me in tight
If only I had a friend at school
If only I had some money to go to the shopping mall
If only I had some nice food
If only I had a brother and sister to play with me
At least one that liked me
If only I had some nice clothes
If only I had a nice-looking pose
If only I could go to some really good fun places
If only I had some laces.

Rudy Singh (9)
Eagle House School, Sandhurst

A Nightmare

In darkness I must walk cautiously
Be as silent as death
Living in the ruined house
Damp rooms.

Heard screaming, shouting and killing
My lovely life is gone
Far, far away.

I want to play with my dog
Friends and family
Talking, singing and dancing
Lie down and look at sunshine
Listen to the birds singing
Christmas parties with friends, carols . . .
Have my lovely life again.

Nancy Kang
Eagle House School, Sandhurst

The Years Of Misery

Dark and hopeless
My glum heart
Waits for light to break through
And end this suffering.

I long to leap about our house
Yodel and chant
Play games and puzzles
Bounce on trampolines
Perform in a play
Run a race, sit on a horse
Rush in the wind, howl with the wolves.

Charlie Riddell & Thor Winkler von Stioernhielm (10)
Eagle House School, Sandhurst

Nightmare

In dark and silent rooms
We whisper to each other
The smell of death all around outside
Lonely, scary days, round and round
But we can't throw away the hope
We are waiting for freedom.

I hope this is a nightmare
With bright sunshine when I wake up
Through the window
To light up my skin
Long happy days to pass by
I hope this is a nightmare.

Yuna Kojima (11)
Eagle House School, Sandhurst

Angler Fish

Far beneath the quivering waves
Near the bottom of the ocean
Inky and moonless
It drifts silently
Scanning for victims like an assassin
Displaying its glowing danger
Dangerous predator
Of the
Deep
Dark
Deep.

Ben Moore (9)
Eagle House School, Sandhurst

The Crocodile

As you creep along, slow and steadily
With your scales rough like concrete
Your big eyes yellow and green
Submerging into the water, you watch
Everything going by
Razor teeth
Needle-sharp
Silent and motionless
Ready to pounce.

Laura Neat (9)
Eagle House School, Sandhurst

Giraffe

Skin like brown pebbles on the beach
Giant of the African savannah
Striding steadily
Long violet tongue seizing
Emerald-green leaves
Spotty tail swinging
Side to side.

Tanaquille Manton-Jones & Ashley Inglis (9)
Eagle House School, Sandhurst

Snow Leopard

Flying off the rock
Landing on four paws
Pouncing forward to grab its prey
A growling purr of pleasure
Withdrawing slowly
Gracefully
Blending back into the wintry backdrop.

Mohammed Rubbani (9)
Eagle House School, Sandhurst

The Secret Annexe

Creeping over ancient floorboards
Wandering words
Longing, wondering
Living life, but
Waiting . . . waiting . . . waiting

I want to run over this wooden floor
I want to enjoy life as it comes
Coming and going as I please
Playing with Mother Nature
Hoping . . . hoping . . . hoping.

Ross Pawley-Kean (10)
Eagle House School, Sandhurst

Ant Army

In single file they march silently
Towards their assignment
Countless legs
Striding side by side
A noiseless, armoured war tank
They work together like a military unit.

Harry Baldock (9)
Eagle House School, Sandhurst

Scorpion

There you tread
Buried in bushes
In your metallic armour
Moving concealed
Scuttling in your tracks
A deadly tail
Yellow beady eyes
Checking your way.

Adam Robinson (9)
Eagle House School, Sandhurst

The Secret Annexe

Still they tiptoed silently over the creaky floorboards
Silent words
Living in the darkness of the claustrophobic rooms
Weeks pass, feeling more frightened every day
Hoping and waiting.

I want to run and jump on the floor
Shout in laughter
Rip back the windows
Tear back the curtains
But still hoping.

Reece Williams (10)
Eagle House School, Sandhurst

Dainty Dolphin

Your rubbery grey skin like polished leather
Gliding through the deep blue sea
Occasionally leaping in and out
Squeaking like a knotted throat
You play with a pod of friends
Until the day ends.

Aanya Das & Maggie Knox (9)
Eagle House School, Sandhurst

Crab

He is munchy to eat
Because he has lots of meat
His shell is very hard like a giant card
You can only see him on the beach rocks
You may see him lots and lots
He is gentle, he is mental
He will nip you, he will clip you if you are vicious
I am sorry, but he will.

Eleisha Lockwood (8)
Elham CE Primary School, Canterbury

The Blue Rocket

Pilots hoping to find good sights
When they check the world
Racing with their friends
And flying together forever
Zooming from planet to planet
Meeting each other at different places
Flying through the mist like a shooting star
Rockets zooming and blazing
Even diving, spinning and twirling
Trying to find out about the Earth.

Annie Gower (7)
Elham CE Primary School, Canterbury

Tree

Rustling, outspread
Like a green giant
Branches wave in the wind
Leaves change colour in the winter
You become multicoloured
New buds grow in the spring
Branches bare in the winter like a wooden skeleton
Tree trunk brown and rough like a grizzly bear.

William Herbert (8)
Elham CE Primary School, Canterbury

My Beautiful Dog

His coat is fluffy and warm
He likes me because he loves me
A beautiful dog
I hug my dog because he is precious to me
He looks nice and black
He is covered in fur.

Alexandria Willoughby (7)
Elham CE Primary School, Canterbury

Colourful Rainbow

Sparkling, shimmering rainbow I love
I can't take my eyes off it
It's way too smooth. Shining, reflecting from the river
Such beautiful colours
Red, orange, yellow, blue, indigo and violet
Sparkling in the sun colourful colours shine
It only comes up when the sun and rain are together
Over the rainbow I go to find the treasure
In the end I'm bringing back to my family
So we will be rich
When I opened it, it had jewels and diamonds
It was so exciting!

Tara Woodley (7)
Elham CE Primary School, Canterbury

Lightning

Lightning flashing like fire
Lightning trying to find a path to Earth
Lightning as big as Kent
White lightning
Blue lightning
Yellow lightning
Bolt of raw electrical power.

Faris Cooke (8)
Elham CE Primary School, Canterbury

Sebastian Snake

I am Sebastian Snake
I am gooey and sticky
Slimy and I have one big foot
Boom, if I bite and gobble my prey
I live forever
If I live up to 100
I munch and crunch
I am as slow as a snail
At one mile per hour
I take ages to eat
Bold and bright in colour
I sleep like a mouse
In a big pack of grass.

Isobel Van Eerten (7)
Elham CE Primary School, Canterbury

Guitar

Hand playing as quick as lightning
Silver amp hard as a skull from a badger
A heavy case is shiny wood
Six strings to pluck
Deep low notes
A book full of music
I love my guitar.

Ben Lewis (8)
Elham CE Primary School, Canterbury

What Was It?

I saw a blur rushing by
It sped past as fast as a cheetah
What was it?

I thought and thought
What could it be?
Could it be a car?
Could it be a truck?
Could it be a van?
Could it be my friend Dan?

Another blur came rushing by
I thought again over and over
I carried on thinking
But I could not work out what it could be.

James Lindsay (8)
Elham CE Primary School, Canterbury

Earring

It hangs on people's ears
Its colour, yellow and green and purple
When you have your ears pierced
It hurts a bit.

Diamond like a block of ice
My earring is very precious
Very precious
Sometimes you don't wear your earrings
Sparkly, small, white, beautiful
My earrings are lovely.

Lily Theoff (7)
Elham CE Primary School, Canterbury

Burning Forest

I see flames burning bright
I see shining colours
What is it?

I smell leaves burning fast
I smell smoke very strongly
I wonder what it is?

I hear crackling trees
I hear sirens rushing all around
What am I?
Fire!

Ellie Pettit (8)
Elham CE Primary School, Canterbury

Sunset

I wish I was at the beach
I would look at fish swimming around my feet
The pink sky with fluffy clouds
The waves jiggling and dancing away
Every time they come and sway
I wish I was at the beach
To be where sea and sky meet
Swim down to the ocean floor
To gather pearls and much, much more.

Fergus Dougal (8)
Elham CE Primary School, Canterbury

Santa Claus

With eyes a-twinkling
Red cheeks glowing
A-racing through the sky
Came Santa Claus,
Yes, Santa Claus a-racing through the sky.

Sailing over mountains
Flying over seas
Giving out presents for everyone to see
Came Santa Claus,
Yes, Santa Claus with presents for us to see.

There's a chubby man,
Yes, a chubby man a-racing through the sky
Delivering presents to everyone who's full of apple pie.

It's Santa Claus I tell you
It's Santa Claus I said
It's Santa Claus I screamed aloud
I hear him overhead.

Charlotte Harbour (9)
Elham CE Primary School, Canterbury

Spring

Standing in a meadow by a stream
I can see bunnies hopping in the bluebells
And trees blowing in the wind
I can smell flowers with a lovely scent
I can touch the jewelled grass and pine needles
I can taste the honey from a beehive
It tastes like caramel from a chocolate factory.

Alex Hannah (8)
Elham CE Primary School, Canterbury

The Volcano's Heat

The heat is full of power
I feel myself going down, down, down
Deeper into the hot silky lava
I felt like a baby potato
Shrivelling into a ball of ash.

My heart is racing
I tried to stay up above the lava
But I couldn't
It felt like strong hands were pulling me down
But when I tried to kick
It was no use, the lava was too thick.

I stopped to listen
I yelled, 'Help me someone.'
But then out of nowhere
First came a rumble, then a tumble
I felt myself fly up into the air
Lava flinging everywhere
At last I could go home.

Emily Andrews (9)
Elham CE Primary School, Canterbury

Kangaroo

Kangaroos jump and bounce
They are very clever and very silly
I think about kangaroos in the wild
And it would mean a lot to me
If I saw one because I like them so much.

Lauren-Amy Lord (7)
Elham CE Primary School, Canterbury

The Ice Valley

The silvery silky footpath
In the white, white snow
Leading to the igloo where the polar bears hide

The velvet sea like a pool
Where the icy icebergs are
The icy footprints on the stepping stones
Like the animal is leading the way

The ice melts nicely touching
To just squeeze a footpath in-between
The wind is whistling calmly
Making it almost silent
The clouds passing by
Making a slight sound of a CD playing
A rain stick that sounds like clouds

The jiggly fish jumping in and out of their hole
Making the polar bears hungry when they jump
The trees are covered in snow
But don't mind, they just stand there
Thinking that they don't care.

The red sky at dusk leading to sunset
The blue sky fades
It is getting colder now the day has gone.

This all happened in Iceland.

Lucy Barnes (9)
Elham CE Primary School, Canterbury

The Jungle Coaster

Wake up, wake up, we've got to get going
I get out of bed excited but yawning
Long journey in the dark, we're off
To our favourite park.

Arriving at the gate we pay to get in
And get an inky stamp on our skin
Smells of hot dogs, taste of ice cream
Chips and burgers, ice cream and I scream
The dragon, the splash, the whirly spider
And now the big one, the Jungle Coaster
Click-clack, click-clack
As the car goes up the track
We laugh with a nervous sound
Then scream as we rush towards the ground
Daddy says, 'It's OK, it's OK,' then starts to cry
As we whoop and laugh and touch the sky
Up and down, round and round
Bash and crash, so far from the ground
Daddy grips the bar and seems in pain
As we scream, 'Again, again!'

Ride's over, get an ice cream to lick
Apart from Daddy who feels sick?
But drives us back and into bed
And gets a tablet for his head.

William Turnbull (9)
Elham CE Primary School, Canterbury

My Tornado Dream

As I played in a field below the mountains
I saw a swirl of wind and heard a whistle
Suddenly I saw a tornado
It came nearer and nearer
I ran back to the house
But the wind pulled me back
I couldn't see anything
It was all a blur
And in the distance
I just spotted a tree
I ran over and clung to the tree
The tornado pulled my hands free
The next thing I knew
I was in my house
I woke up and looked out the window
But the tornado wasn't there.

Jerra Wooding (10)
Elham CE Primary School, Canterbury

What Am I?

I don't eat meat
I have a bright coat
I have a sharp beak
I am a small bird
I live in trees
I fly
What am I?

David Willoughby (8)
Elham CE Primary School, Canterbury

I Wonder What it Is?

I hear a bang
I see a spark
I wonder what it is?

Red, blue, green and gold
Shimmering in the velvet sky
I wonder what it is?

My heart is beating with excitement
Crackle, bang, oh the noise
I wonder what it is?

What is it?
What is it?
It is a firework!

Sabrina Cook (8)
Elham CE Primary School, Canterbury

On The Way To Church

The bells are ringing
The children are singing
On the way to church.

The snow is falling
With excitement my heart is beating
On the way to church.

My dad is smiling
My mum is crying
On the way to church.

What is happening?
The baby is giggling because of the christening
On the way to church.

Eliza Gammon (10)
Elham CE Primary School, Canterbury

Autumn Spirits

A calling in the distance
A whispering muffled and faint
O'er the ground the trees bare, bow down
All in a beautiful sunset in the evening, very late.

Forlorn in the silence
An ambience of mystical cry
And russet crisp leaf falls off the trees
And autumn spirits whisper where they fly.

Gliding wisps of moonlight
Shine the leaves silver in silver shoon
Yet the spirits sigh their lonely song
Their autumn distant tune.

Cold and calm and breezy
Looming shadows ask
In the autumn winds so hazy
But what do the autumn winds hold?
What is to be foretold?
Is what the autumn spirits ask
And all will be revealed in the future
Yet the present, although it is the past.

Eleanor Hart-Dyke (9)
Elham CE Primary School, Canterbury

Fireworks

F ireworks sizzling, hissing, spluttering
I watch the perilous display of vibrant colour bursts
R esounding, thunderous, ear-splitting noises
E asily phenomenal mind-boggling spectacles
W olfing down scrumptious tomato soup
O dours of burning gunpowder making you cough and splutter
R ed, yellow, green and blue, a multicoloured sight, a
K aleidoscope which lights up the sky
S orrowful to leave I'll be, but I'm back again next year.

Rosie Rutherford (9)
Elham CE Primary School, Canterbury

Hallowe'en

Every year at Hallowe'en my friends and I go out
We like to do a trick or treat, we laugh, we scream, we shout.

On our street there's a great big house that's old and huge and creaky
We scare ourselves by going there, cos it's really, really freaky.

We knock on the door, then run away in case a ghost appears
My friend falls down, his torch goes out, it's dark, my greatest fear.

We reach a cottage up a lane and knock loudly on the door
A witch says, 'Welcome boys, please do come in,'
Then knocks us to the floor.

She raised her wand and chants a spell and Sam becomes a frog
Ben is turned into a pig and I'm a growling dog.

We run away to safety, to a large and friendly house
We are given mugs of cocoa and a lovely chocolate mouse.

Max Wren (9)
Elham CE Primary School, Canterbury

Skiing Mayhem

Lost your ski on the lift
Too big and fat you've got to shift.

Got to the top, there's no way back
Too steep for you, well look at that!

Get back on the lift, we're going right to the top
Don't need any money, there is no shop.

There's a restaurant up there with a very nice view
Well, it is for the French but I don't know about you.

It's a beautiful view, now I think that I'm French
Ow, now I've lost my keys, they're over there on the bench!

Francesca Godden (8)
Elham CE Primary School, Canterbury

Nightmares

I had a dream that dark, dark night
When all the world was sleeping
I stepped inside the gloom
And there the man was waiting
The master of disguise, the threat inside his eyes
I had a dream that dark, dark night
The castle as cold as ice
The scuttling of the tiny mice
The curious man was walking towards me on the creaky floor
I ran towards the odd-shaped door
I heard screaming below the floor.

I had a dream that dark, dark night
When all the world was sleeping
The wolves were howling in my mind
My heart started thumping
There was creeping up my spine.

I had a dream that dark, dark night
When all the world was sleeping.

Megan Rutherford (9)
Elham CE Primary School, Canterbury

Sweets

Too many sweets to tempt my mind
The yummiest sweet I have to find
Chocolate buttons in my mouth beginning to melt
Gobbling them down one by one
Fat Maltesers teasing my tongue
With one big crunch my teeth attack
Lovely liquorice all shiny and black
Fizzy Cola bottles make me squint and squirm
Long, thin, chewy and gooey are strawberry worms
I just don't know what to choose
It's so easy to be confused
But my favourite by far
Is a chocolate Galaxy bar.

Sam Pratt (9)
Elham CE Primary School, Canterbury

My Pet Maggot, Ricky

My pet maggot, Ricky
He's my best ever friend
I nurse him when he's sicky
I'll love him till the end.

My pet maggot, Ricky
He goes everywhere with me
I take him to my school each day
He fills me with smiles and glee.

My pet maggot, Ricky
He does annoy my mum
He's always eating all the food
To stop his rumbling tum.

Lotty Astbury (9)
Elham CE Primary School, Canterbury

Dog

Three-legged scratching, scritch, scratch, scritch, scratch
Play, play, play, play.
Non-stop sniffing, snuffle, sniffle, snuffle
Play, play, play, play.
Tail like a flag, wag, wag, wag
Play, play, play, play.
Tongue lolling, slather, dribble, slobber
Play, play, play, play.
Radar ears, twitch, twitch, twitch
Play, play, play, play.
Please play with me!

Jacob Glass (9)
Elham CE Primary School, Canterbury

Autumn

People wearing gloves and hats
Happy in the garden
Tyre swing on the tree
Children playing in the leaves
Crunch, crunch, crunch they go.

Rabbits thumping on the ground
And playing all around
Squirrels running up the trees
And collecting nuts and berries.

Wind blowing in my hair
Running about without a care
Splashing in the puddles
Out in the street
Then Mum cooking apple pie
For me to eat.

Elanah Harvey (9)
Elham CE Primary School, Canterbury

Scaly Creature

In the cold night you might shiver
The creature might be there
Along the floor it will slither
So you must beware.

It will slither across the street
In the midnight sky
It will always get you
Even if you try.

If it sees you just relax
Do not move even a bit
Be extremely careful
And watch out, he might spit.

Abigail Connor (10)
Highfield School, Maidenhead

Tiger

The vicious tiger roaring loudly
As the night is drawing in
It hunts about for rats and mice
Scaring birds and angry beasts.

Goes to sleep in crack of dawn
Wakes up with a squeak and yawn
It looks, it looks and what it sees
A mouse, a mouse, with hairs and fleas.

Eats it up and looks around
The friend of the mouse it has found
Walks around the jungle floors
With his mum who he adores.

Hunts about in summer
Hunts about in spring
Hunts about in autumn
And in winter when he's king!

Alexandra Wilcox (10)
Highfield School, Maidenhead

The Clever Rat

The rattlesnake slithers through the moonlight
As he gives all a huge fright
Rattling a graceful tune
He gazes up at the moon.

I could see his scaly skin
As he approached the rusty tin
He waited for his prey
To come out anytime his way.

At long last a rat appears
In his eyes you could see his tears
The snake gets ready to kill
But the rat has too much skill!

Elnaz Bedroud (10)
Highfield School, Maidenhead

Seasons

I like it in the summer
When the sun shines down on me
I like it when we go and stay near by the sea
I like it when there is no school
I also love to jump in the pool.

But then it gets a bit colder
And that's when autumn arrives
Autumn's my favourite season
But that is no surprise
The leaves crackle below my feet
The gold leaves are such a treat
With red, yellow, orange and brown
Autumn is nature's gown.

Then it's winter, the season of snow
It's fun when Father Christmas comes
Flying with a glow
He brings me lots of presents
Stockings loaded with things
I always wake up early and see what he brings.

Then in the spring the snow clears away
Flowers bloom, four every day
The animals are born, *hip hip hooray!*
Then it gets hotter, summer's here again
Now it's time to happen all over again.

Eleanor Slade (10)
Highfield School, Maidenhead

The Moonlit Alps

Deep in the heart of the moonlit Alps
The creatures of the night are starting to come out
Beneath the ocean of glistening stars
You can only just see the planet Mars.

A herd of horses comes to graze
But swiftly gallop back through this maze
At last they all decide to go
Leaving the mountain covered in snow.

The mountain is silver, the mountain is gold
The mountain is over one hundred years old
Its face is truly covered in trees
With an icy wind cold enough to freeze.

Left alone in the midnight's wrath
Left to play with the smallest moth
That is the tale of the moonlit Alps
Where the creatures of the night are starting to come out.

Maddie Merryweather (10)
Highfield School, Maidenhead

Pencil Case

There is a small old pencil case
A-sitting on my desk
The secrets hiding inside it
No one could possibly guess.

Inside this small old pencil case
Are elves and fairies with wings
Running and jumping and moving about
Fixing a thousand things.

When your pencil case is closed
They sprint and leap and play
But when you open your pencil case
They quickly run away.

Elsa Desmond (10)
Highfield School, Maidenhead

Christmas Morning

Wake up early, Christmas is here
Look out the window to see snow appear
It's magic, I shout, 'I'm going out!'
As I step through the door, I have to see more
As I trudge through the snow, I never wanted it to go
I sprinted to the shed, hidden behind the snowy hedge
I jump around with excitement as I get out the sled
Snow glinting like a diamond in the sun's rays
Peeking through the crack of the cloud
Snow piled high on the garden wall
Then I see something that catches my eye, glittering in the hall
It's a sack full of presents, I call, 'Look at them all.'
I got some sweeties, some chocolate and a cuddly teddy bear
Some new clothes, a bracelet and a brush for my hair
I had a Christmas of long happy days with family and friends
I'll treasure it always.

Alice Lineham (10)
Highfield School, Maidenhead

Crunch! Crunch!

Crunch! Crunch!
Go the leaves on an autumn day
Wrapped up in scarf and coat I hear them as I play.

Autumn leaves are rusty brown and golden reds -
I see them falling past my window as I lie in bed.

Crisp, dry and shrivelled the leaves are on the ground;
I rake them up, every one into a little mound.

Skeleton leaves are crackling on the fire
The flames are burning red and gold;
They seem to be telling me stories, yet untold!

Catrin Williams (9)
Highfield School, Maidenhead

Anger

When I am angry
I feel like a red-hot chilli pepper sizzling in a frying pan
Anger tastes like burning hot volcano lava
Spreading across your tongue
It sounds like a deafening screech of nails down a blackboard
It smells like burnt black toast creeping up through your nostrils.

Anger lives in the deepest darkest forest
Trying to destroy all the calmness and happiness out of your heart
It likes to hang around with fury and rage, teasing all the other feelings
Anger moves like a fire-breathing dragon
Trampling all the houses in the village
Anger destroys everything around it
And you must not let it into your heart.

Olivia Thomson (10)
Highfield School, Maidenhead

Happiness

Happiness feels like the sunlight
It tastes like melted chocolate
It sounds like a choir singing
It looks like a smiling face.

It smells like a field of lavender
It lives in your heart and soul
It is multicoloured just like a rainbow
It enjoys singing and dancing under the moon.

Lily Streames-Smith (10)
Highfield School, Maidenhead

Emerald Eyes

Knock, knock
Tack, tick
On the ceiling
Again and again

I crept out of bed
And up the old creaky staircase
Knock, knock
Tack, tick.

I opened the door to the loft
Eeek!
Argh!
I screamed.

Emerald eyes stared at me
A beast's eyes
Looking at me
My heart leapt into my mouth.

I looked down at my kitten's bed
Whiskers was gone!
Miaow, miaow
I looked at the emerald-eyed beast
Whiskers!

Alexandra Kirkup-Lee (11)
Highfield School, Maidenhead

Biscuits, Biscuits, Biscuits

Ginger biscuits
Chewy biscuits
Big, fat, chocolate biscuits
Golden, yellow, shortbread biscuits
Those are just a few.

Digestive biscuits
Bourbon biscuits
Big, fat, creamy biscuits
Very tasty Hob Nob biscuits
Lots more too.

Big biscuits
Small biscuits
Even little doggy biscuits
Last of all, best of all
I like home-made biscuits!

Alice Armstrong (9)
Highfield School, Maidenhead

Wishes

Can wishes come true
Or can they not?
I made a wish last night and said,
'Starlight, star bright
First star I see tonight
I wish I may
I wish I might
Have the wish I wish tonight.'
My wish came true
Now I do believe in wishes
I hope you do too.

Jaipreet Kaur Banwaith (8)
Highfield School, Maidenhead

Spicy Chilli

Spicy chilli hot
Spicy chilli in the pot
Everyone who likes this meal called spicy chilli
Has a name that rhymes with silly
Spicy chilli hot, spicy chilli cold
Spicy chilli nine weeks old
My mum will eat it, I will not
Do you know, it gets my intestines in a knot
Bubble, bubble
Boil, boil
I know what's in that pot -
Don't tell me it's not that spicy chilli meal
I can't believe it passed my mum's taste appeal
Now came the dreaded time
Dinnertime of course
I tried that meal, it was not subtle
It was not calm
So I turned on my body's fire alarm
Bubble, bubble
Plop, splat, oh drat
That rat, it ate spicy chilli off my plate
And now I don't have to eat the meal I hate!

Sarah Williams (8)
Highfield School, Maidenhead

Family And Friends

Loving family, happy friends
Playing together that never ends
Kissing goodnight, saying goodbye
Telling stories and singing lullabies.

Caring family, lovely home
Full with love, never alone
Mum and Dad, brothers and sisters
Helping each other and sharing joy.

Helpful friends, wonderful school
Swimming in the turquoise pool
Different people from all around the world
Making new mates and learning things.

Teachers are bossy, teachers are kind
But they are helping you even if you're behind
Parents tell you off and even given you food
But you still love them too.

Karina Law (9)
Highfield School, Maidenhead

Chug, Chug, Chug

Clickety, clackety, clickety, clackety
Choo-choo, chug, chug
Here we go, we're going today
We're going away, away, away
The train's whistling, hissing along the iron rails
Shovel the coal, shovel the coal;
It's getting hotter, hotter, hotter
We're building up, we're going to blow
Swooooosh
Chug, chug
We're slowing down
We're here!

Paven Uppal (10)
Highfield School, Maidenhead

Sweets, Sweets, Sweets

Jelly beans
Lemon sherbet
Small round bonbon sweet
Long thin liquorice sweets
Brown Coca-Cola sweets
These are just a few
Mint sweets
Lip sweets
Big gobstopper sweets
Square Starburst sweets
Soft marshmallow sweets too
Heart sweets
Lolly sweets
Don't forget the pear sweets
Last of all, best of all
I like milk sweets.

Jodie Passmore (9)
Highfield School, Maidenhead

A Splash Of Sun

Sunny games
In funny caves

Sandy shells
In summer bells

Seaside fun
Is soon begun

Running free
Laughing with glee

Sunset beach
Within my reach.

Carmen Roca-Igual (9)
Highfield School, Maidenhead

Fish, Fish, Fish

Haddock fish
Sei fish
Very oily salmon fish
Rosy-pink prawn fish
Those are just a few.

Cod fish
Mackerel fish
Multicoloured trout fish
Blue-shelled mussel fish
Flying fish too.

Squid fish
Puffer fish
Don't forget the jellyfish
Last of all, best of all
I like swordfish.

Tia Folley (9)
Highfield School, Maidenhead

Strange Horse

Swishy tail
Pink body
Purple hooves
Wings as big as an eagle's
Do you know what this creature is?
Horse head
Weird ears
Great hearing of this creature
I give you a clue, it does not wear shoes
Mythical creature
Not real
But it's a flying horse
It's Pegasus!

Natashia Berrio (8)
Highfield School, Maidenhead

Spring

Spring has come
And in this season
Lots of birds like to hum.

Baby animals are being born
Learning to walk
Trotting on the warm, green lawn.

Daffodils, primroses
Bloom to breathe the fresh air of spring
And are watered by hoses.

Feathery birds
Hum songs of joy
Making sure everyone has heard.

Happy folks
Having picnics together
Under the same shady oak.

And just around the corner
Is summer.

Annabel Chan (9)
Highfield School, Maidenhead

Autumn

Autumn's arrived, you can tell it's here,
Leaves golden-brown, men brewing beer.
There's a cold nip in the air, fires are lit,
But that doesn't matter a single bit.
The sound of children, kicking up leaves,
Leaves are swirling, caught on the breeze.
Autumn's arrived, you can tell it's here.

Florence Weaver (9)
Highfield School, Maidenhead

Cake, Cake, Cake!

Carrot cake
Lemon cake
Nice, tasty, fruity cake
Very filling, treacle cake
Those are just a few
Ginger cake
Scone cake
Lovely, sweet, cupcakes
Decorative cake too
Wedding cake
Sponge cake
Don't forget the iced cake
Last of all, best of all
I like chocolate cake!

Georgina Lockwood (9)
Highfield School, Maidenhead

That's What Our Lion Does

There is a lion on the plains
Padding softly towards the village -
Is it going to eat us or love us?

Nobody knows, just me
It's going to love us like a cat
Not eat us like a bear.

With its long flowing mane
He stalks his prey -
A giraffe, an antelope maybe.

He chases his prey to catch it
Tear it up and eat it
That's what our lion does.

Catherine Tren (9)
Highfield School, Maidenhead

A Day At The Beach

I wake up early
Dawn is fading fast
Bright blue skies are coming.

I pack my bag
Down the stairs
Then I go running.

Here at last, not alone
People all about
Having fun in the sun - there's no doubt.

Running in the summer sun
Soft white sand to land on.

Going in the deep blue sea
As cold as can be.

Getting dressed one more time
The day has ended, home once again.

Rebecca Duffey (9)
Highfield School, Maidenhead

Winter's Coming

Summer's fallen, winter's arrived
Leaves are rustling, plants have died.
Rain is falling beneath my feet
Winter's arrival is almost complete.
Chilly days come before us
Put on your coats, get on the school bus.
Snowflakes form on frosty windows
Announcing the arrival of winter snows
Summer's fallen, winter's arrived
Leaves are rustling, plants have died.
But I am still in summer, I am still in heat
But my house is covered in a cold white sheet.

Alice Slade (9)
Highfield School, Maidenhead

They Tell Me

They tell me to be a dog
Fast and leapy
I tell them I want to be a cat
Slow and sleepy.

They tell me to be a horse
Energetic and fun
I tell them I want to be an ant
Dead asleep.

They tell me to be an angel
Holy and sweet
I tell them I want to be a devil
Cheeky and deep.

They tell me to be the sun
Joyful and caring
I tell them I want to be lightning and thunder
Mean and scaring.

Mollie O'Flaherty (9)
Highfield School, Maidenhead

Autumn Has Begun

I was walking through a path
On a lovely summer's morning
The sun was shimmering in the summer sky.

As I was strolling along the path
I saw children playing and racing in the fields
Everyone eating lunch in the sun outside.

Everywhere was busy
Everyone in the gleaming sunshine
Ice creams melting and spilling everywhere.

Suddenly it got cooler, the sun had gone
The leaves were shaking
Autumn had begun!

Elika Bedroud (9)
Highfield School, Maidenhead

The Sunset Unicorn

Night again, sunset soon rushing towards the hilltop
Sun slowly going down, bright light shining all around
Going into the sky, it's like a firefly -
Fire flames orange, red, yellow too
Dashing right into the sky
Suddenly, as the unicorn went into the sky
The sky flashes bright as the sunset
Lit up bright then goes midnight.

The two secret unicorns
Running, running to the hilltops
Galloping all the way
The purple sky, flying high into the sky
As sparkles dash behind them
Dashing purple flames down into the sky
Playing, galloping and jumping over each other
Until black as midnight.

Sophie Bujakowski (8)
Highfield School, Maidenhead

Winter Days

Stalactites hanging from the gutter
Running water stopped as ice
Snowflakes falling to the icy ground
Children wrapped up in a satin gown
Mums and dads drinking steamy-hot tea
Making snowmen - how much fun it can be
At night children sitting by the fire
Children practising their own lure
Families standing around the Christmas tree singing joyful songs
People in their cosy beds with the long nights
On Christmas Day children eating roast lunch
A touch of gravy to top it all up.

Kamini Khindria (9)
Highfield School, Maidenhead

Sweets, Sweets, Sweets

Milky sweets
Crunchy sweets
Long, thin, pretty sweets
Big, fat, smelly sweets
Those are just a few
Brown sweets
Coloured sweets
Big, fat, killer sweets
Brown, cold, icy sweets
Skipping sweets too
Long sweets
Big sweets
Don't forget Christmas sweets
Last of all, best of all
I like chocolate sweets.

Sweta Pradeepkumar (8)
Highfield School, Maidenhead

Dragons

Hot flames
Burning trees
Scarlet night
Dragon's eye
A scaly body creeps along the damp grass
Dark and scarlet dragons' caves
Lit with a fire-breathing dragon
Dragons go hunting as midnight strikes
Hunting for rabbits and hares
Swooping high, swooping low
Roar, roar
Fire going everywhere, over here and over there
Walking back to his cave, a dragon sleeps there so
Beware!

Ruby Griffiths (9)
Highfield School, Maidenhead

Christmas Presents

On Christmas Eve
You sit and wait
Wondering what presents you will get
Later that night
The flight of Santa begins
Next morning you wake up
And look at your stocking excitedly
It is filled with lovely gifts
You run into your mum's room
And *jump on her!*
Run downstairs and open your presents
Thanks for the presents
Can I have some breakfast?
When I've opened all my presents
The bag of rubbish is full
My cat climbs into it and gets stuck
She walks around, the bag on her head
We think that she's a monster
And we run around instead.
The time has come to eat the turkey
And the roast potato
Pour the gravy
Eat the peas
Then go into the kitchen
Fetch the Christmas pudding and the chocolate log
Eat the log, enjoy them a lot
Then comes the afternoon, sun shining brightly
Time to play with your presents and watch a Christmas movie
I had a wonderful Christmas
It will be a memory.

Katie Parry (9)
Highfield School, Maidenhead

Ponies

Star is black with a white star
Muffin has a cheeky grin
Magic is grey with little black ears
And Fairy has tiny twinkly hooves
Angel likes to fly through the air
The grass is greener for Betty over the fence
And Fly's coat is soft as silk
But King is the naughtiest one.

All the ponies meet at the gymkhana
The sun is bright
The ponies' coats shine in the sun
Their tails are plaited and they are ready to run.

The walk and trot race is hard for King
But the egg and spoon race is great for Star
Magic gets excited and canters afar
Muffin's rider falls off at a turn
Fairy and her rider are about to part
Fly rears as he is waiting to start
Angel holds the lead across the line
Betty finds it too much hard work.

But everyone has such a fun time
Prizes and rosettes are won
It's time to go home and feed the performers
Tucked in their stables and said goodnight.

Esme O'Sullivan (8)
Highfield School, Maidenhead

My Pets

My cat is very hairy
Especially when he is untidy
He can dance like a ballerina
With pretty frilly knickers
And red lipstick too
Including mascara
That is enough today
I'll tell you about my dog

My dog is very scary
Especially when he is lazy
He cannot dance like a ballerina
With no frilly knickers
But red lipstick too
Never ever forget mascara
That is enough today
I'll tell you about my bunny.

My bunny is very shy
When you peep at him he will cry
When he runs his tail will go up and down
My bunny is so cute he will cuddle you when you toot.

Rebecca Clark (8)
Highfield School, Maidenhead

Snow!

Dazzling snow
Crunching footsteps
Painted white trees in the gleaming sun
Pitter-patter, on my windowpane
Another joyful day to ski
On the powdery mountain slopes.

Lucy Drew (9)
Highfield School, Maidenhead

Animals Rule

A naconda slithering, sliding on a rock, slide, slither slide
N ewborn rabbit hiding in the burrow, afraid and scared
I n the sea is a fish going swish, swosh, swish, swosh
M y cat likes to scratch like a lion getting ready to catch
A grizzly bear will scare me but it's fine
L eopard in Africa lazing around purring happily
S uperb cheetah running fast, sleek and smooth

R aging monkeys in the treetops screaming
U nable to fly, the penguin goes a long way, wiggle
L emurs are sweet but very energetic
E agles fly so very high and they are very sweet.

Rhianna Cross (8)
Highfield School, Maidenhead

The Witch

This witch is very ugly
They can make themselves very cuddly
They turn children into mice
They are not very nice.

They are always women
They want to kill your sins from birth
When they find you they say, 'Kill them!'
They are the creepiest on the Earth.

Jamie Nichols (11)
Kingsnorth CE Primary School, Ashford

The Big Blue

T ough and blue, big and rough
H eroic and dangerous, calm and friendly
E normous sea, tiny boats, endangered species with oil roaming free

B ig and exciting with joyful water
I sle Of Wight and the English Channel
G ulls, whales, rainbow fish, all the amazing animals

S uch big waves with a very big sea
E xciting for children also adults too
A n exciting place is the big blue sea.

Connor Robbins (10)
Kingsnorth CE Primary School, Ashford

The Witch

Her nose is like a knife
And her teeth are evil
And she can turn you into an ugly beetle.

She can kill you before you can say a word
You die by getting burnt
And you'll also be her roast turkey.

Daniel Holland (10)
Kingsnorth CE Primary School, Ashford

The Grand High Witch

A witch is as green as grass
You'll never know when they pass
Make sure you're aware
Or you could be anywhere
They turn you into mice
Which is not very nice.

Orla McGlone (10)
Kingsnorth CE Primary School, Ashford

The Grand High Witch

Witches are ugly, revolting and mean
When a lady comes up to you don't be so keen
She'll bubble you up and seer you for sure
Or she'll try to make you something brand new

Witches are horrible so be aware
When something goes wrong try not to be there
Because you will be next take it from me
Cause I got turned into a big brown tree.

Hannah Terry (11)
Kingsnorth CE Primary School, Ashford

The Romantic Sea

The waves are as soft as silk
Beautiful little boats decorated with pink, red and white lights
The yellow sand crumbles between my toes
The tide washes the sand out of them, it feels so lovely
The sight of the beautiful sea makes my heart melt
If only I could go back to the sea again.

Emma Croker (11)
Kingsnorth CE Primary School, Ashford

The Ginormous Sea

The sea is full of sand
It is like a hand grabbing sand
Even a towel can't soak up the sea
All I can see is the sea
The sea gets bigger when it rains
I can't see any land.

William Ashdown (10)
Kingsnorth CE Primary School, Ashford

The Sea

The sea is a sparkling bowl of shimmering diamonds
That shine all day long
Some days she is an uncontrollable lion
Pounding up on the jagged rocks and mountainsides
Other days she is a quiet mouse
Crawling slowly up on the sandy shores then creeps back down
But on her worst days
She takes innocent lives
And swallows them up into her dark, deep, dangerous depths
She is . . .
Unpredictable.

Katie Wright (10)
Kingsnorth CE Primary School, Ashford

The Sea

The sea is a wonderland
An exhilarating creation of nature
Filled with animals from the sea
Distantly you see the countries from far away
But I cannot tell where the sea finishes
And those distant places begin
The waves are a gently wash where I stand and see.

Martin Nichols (11)
Kingsnorth CE Primary School, Ashford

The Sea

The sea is immensely calm
With a soft gentle sway
The sea is a ruthless mass
Of enormous, brutal, blue, sea waves
Giving the essence of aquamarine velvet
Through the enriching experience
Of the glittering gleaming sea.

Melissa Garwood (10)
Kingsnorth CE Primary School, Ashford

The Wonders Of The Sea

The deep blue sea is like a coiled python
Slithering towards a dark gloomy image
He realises the shore is not far away.

The crashing waves break the silence
Of the wet summer sea
As the merciless tide draws in
The visitors get forced away.

Tom Green, Jack Nutley & George Paul
Kingsnorth CE Primary School, Ashford

The Sea

The sun shines on the shimmering sapphires of the blue sea
The gentle waves softly splash the shiny shingle
A lonely seagull glides gracefully over chalky cliffs
Whilst a single sailboat passes over the horizon.

The wind whips across the dark and threatening sea
Waves crash in a frenzy of anger and rage
A lifeboat heads out into the mouth of the monster
A beast awakened and searching for prey.

Olivia Burt (11)
Kingsnorth CE Primary School, Ashford

The Sea

The sea is a powdered-blue mist
Shining and shimmering amongst the sea waves
As it swims gracefully, twirling round and round
To approach its innocent prey.

The sea is a giant pool with foam and crushed rocks
As it drowns the huge boats and ships
Then watches the humans step into the water
For their summertime dip.

Sian Christopher (10)
Kingsnorth CE Primary School, Ashford

The Raging Sea

The sea is a raging lion, furiously darting waves onto opposing rocks
And the faces of loved ones are netted onto them
The salt-filled water is bitter like a lion's tongue
And his manes are crashing waves of power.

The sea is a hungry dog
With clashing teeth like the sea's waves
He uses his boisterous rage to trap innocent beings
In his devastating whirlpool.

And as the waves start to settle
They become fluffy clouds and start to play with humans
On a hot summer's day.

Bradley King (10)
Kingsnorth CE Primary School, Ashford

The Sea

Waves clash like a raging dragon
Heartlessly using its infinite power to destroy innocent lives
Its colossal surface is used to rip defenceless boats apart.

The Atlantic Ocean spreads its lonely chilling ripples
But sometimes its ripples turn wild, destroying everything in sight.

The sea is a comforting cat
That leaps joyfully, it scratches its foe and sinks boats
It plays when it reaches the shore, tumbling and rolling happily.

Josh Wright (11)
Kingsnorth CE Primary School, Ashford

The Grand High Witch

Who is as ugly as a pig?
The grand high witch.
Who always wears a wig?
The grand high witch.
Who has a hunger for children?
The grand high witch.
Who stays in an inn?
The grand high witch.
Stay alert!

Kayleigh Winn (10)
Kingsnorth CE Primary School, Ashford

The Big Blue Sea

The sea is a monstrous panther
That viciously pounces on innocent defenceless prey
But sometimes its nature is as smooth as a glittering, glass lagoon
The sea is an eagle
That gracefully skims the edge of the waves
In search of an innocent swimmer
The sea is a cold-hearted plate
That serves up the warm comforting sunset.

Toby Morris (11)
Kingsnorth CE Primary School, Ashford

The Blue Sea

The scary sea is dangerous, horrendous but fun
Every wave smashes and crashes onto the seashore
Like sea horses foaming at the mouth
The wind is scary, rearing outside
But I am warm and safe here inside.

Dan Bottachi (10)
Kingsnorth CE Primary School, Ashford

The Sea

The sea is like an aggressive tiger
Thrashing his sharp razor teeth
He stalks you like his anonymous dinner
Padding across the gentle beach

Instantly he grabs his prey
Just in time for his dinner
Creeping towards the sandy floor
Getting ready for his calm sleep.

Now he's wondering what will happen next
When the boats and ships all come and take his treasures
And never give them back.

Abigail Brown & Ashleigh Wheal (10)
Kingsnorth CE Primary School, Ashford

The Sea

The sea is an aggressive source of power
With clashing teeth and shaggy jaws
He furiously rips up the hillside
His waves force an immense power
To inflict pain on his prey.

Furiously swirling the saturated ruthless waves
Conjures a brutal amount of water.

Michael Payne (10)
Kingsnorth CE Primary School, Ashford

The Sea

The sea is a scavenging rat
Chewing at the beach and cliffs with his beastly claws
This giant, wavy mass is waiting in the midst
For a swaying fishing trawler
Going through the blue

The sea is a howling wolf
Hunting for fish bones, going through the seaweed
Leaping in time with the windy breeze
The howling seadog moans.

Scott Roper (10)
Kingsnorth CE Primary School, Ashford

The Grand High Witch

Witches are green and really mean
And just keep away if you're not keen
They have snakes for hair (it's quite bare)
All witches really do give a scare!

They turn you into mice
But it's not really nice
Snap, goes the mousetrap
And there goes your life . . .

Natasha Francis (11)
Kingsnorth CE Primary School, Ashford

When You See A Witch

When you see a witch
Jump in a ditch
Run away from her
And get a hitch.

When you see a witch
Run away from her
She says you are a dirty boy
And you say, 'Durr!'

Callum Booth (10)
Kingsnorth CE Primary School, Ashford

Waves

The waves are vicious lions
Who swallow up their prey.
They roam around their territory
Charging straight for their next victim.

I wish I could be like them
So happy and carefree.
I often wonder how they live
And if they are as joyful as us?

Jack Hardy (10)
Kingsnorth CE Primary School, Ashford

The Grand High Witch

Witches are as false as a wig
But they can be anywhere
They have a face like a dried up fig
And they hide deeply in their secret lair.

She has needles in her face
It's definitely not a favour
To keep her mask in place
She needs help from Mr Taylor.

Will Flockett (10)
Kingsnorth CE Primary School, Ashford

What Am I?

High up in the sky
I look down on you
Like a shimmering beam of light
Night and day go by
I'm still there but invisible by day
But at night I shine
Across the world as helpful as ever
I give light.

Louise Rooker (10)
Licensed Victuallers' Junior School, Ascot

The Darkness

The darkness
As dark as a wraith
As powerful as a storm
As deadly as a scorpion
And a desire like a demon
Like a black Sabbath
Predator hunter.

Devon Kivlehan (9)
Licensed Victuallers' Junior School, Ascot

Fireworks

Fireworks sparkle in the sky
Multicoloured sparks of light shoot up to the sky
A flash of colour ignites the midnight sky
Catherine wheels spin crazily, bright and colourful
The colour dims with the night becoming quiet again.

Emily Howell (9)
Licensed Victuallers' Junior School, Ascot

The Moon

The moon, like a giant light bulb
Sometimes on, sometimes off
Shimmering in the dark night
An oversized torch always shining on us
It is the sun at night
Gleaming and shining in the dark
Looks so near, yet so far away
The moon disappears at day or so it seems.

Elizabeth Hamilton (10)
Licensed Victuallers' Junior School, Ascot

Reflections

Like seeing double as if twins
Spoilt as soon as touched
A symmetrical mirror image
A dazzling experience
But water must be still
The calm water catches the image
So you can see the reflection from the sun.

Tara Bharadia (9)
Licensed Victuallers' Junior School, Ascot

Moon

A shimmering bright object in the distance
High in the sky
White as a newborn baby lamb on a clear night
Following me around like the air at night
All day it hides away
Jumping out at dark.

Zoë Carlin (10)
Licensed Victuallers' Junior School, Ascot

Searchlights

Light producer
Enemy finder
Luminous searcher
Black-out destroyer
Bright as a lightning strike
Lights up even the darkest night
Translucent beam
Shape shifter
UFO hunter.

Rory Carmichael & Matthew Rawlinson (10)
Licensed Victuallers' Junior School, Ascot

Moon

As white as a baby lamb
A luminous face
A spy in the sky
She's everywhere
A magic shine
A hidden shadow
A mystery . . .

Alanah Kendall (10)
Licensed Victuallers' Junior School, Ascot

Horrified

I am horrified of scary movies
Long grass terrified of a lawnmower
Swarms of ants fearing the bug spray
Wooden planks fear hacksaws
Guns of glue scared of staplers
Weeds petrified of weed killers
I am horrified of scary movies.

Joseph Moore (10)
Marish Primary School, Slough

Colours Of The Rainbow

I am greeted by colours of the rainbow
Red is like roses, beautiful roses on a fresh clean stalk
Yellow is like the sun as it shines over the lands
Orange is like carrots getting eaten by cute baby rabbits
Green is like the grass growing all light and crunchy
Blue is like the sky, whether it is dark, light or cold
Purple is like juicy plums sitting in a fruit basket
Pink is like clothes, clothes for girls, furry, thin or silk
I am delighted by colours, colours of the rainbow.

Chloe King El-Bokhari (11)
Marish Primary School, Slough

Closeaseparable

I am inseparable from creamy chocolate cake
Like a tree pulled in by its strong roots
Like a road attached to the patterns from the car wheels
Like a literacy lesson with Ms Morgan
Like a TV controlled by a remote with colourful buttons
I am inseparable from chocolate cake.

Scott Hensley (11)
Marish Primary School, Slough

Love

Love is like the colour pink
It smells like a rose petal swaying in the breeze
It tastes like an ice cream with chocolate sprinkles
It looks like two dogs having fun in the sun
It sounds like church bells ringing on Christmas Day.

Clare Highams (11)
Marish Primary School, Slough

Disappointment

Disappointment is blue like the midnight sky
It tastes like ocean water
It smells like a muddy swamp
It looks like a dead tree.

Disappointment sounds like a roar of distress
But feels like a broken nose
If only someone hadn't broken their promise
There wouldn't have been disappointment at all.

Liam Condon (10)
Marish Primary School, Slough

Animals

I am amazed by animals
Like a bee is attracted to honey
Like a bat is blinded by light
Live TVs are fascinated by humans
Like a ball is loved by a footballer
Like a baby delighted by milk
I am amazed by animals.

Ellenna Brooks (11)
Marish Primary School, Slough

Chocolate Addiction

I am addicted to chocolate
Like a book is inspired by a reader
Like a vicar is attached to a church
Like children are attracted to sugar
Like my friend is addicted to his smile
Like paper is inspired with a pen
But I am addicted to chocolate.

Daniel Blanchard (10)
Marish Primary School, Slough

Happiness

Happiness is as bright as the yellow sun
It tastes like hot custard with chocolate cake
It smells like freshly cut grass in a baseball stadium
It looks like the waves in the sea slowly coming towards you
It sounds like beautiful birds flying in the sky
It feels like you have been praised in Heaven.

Sohail Mir (11)
Marish Primary School, Slough

Lonely

Lonely is grey like clouds on a rainy day
It tastes like cold soup
It smells like out of date milk
It looks like an empty street
It sounds like echoing footsteps
It feels like an abandoned damp dog.

Liam Conlon-Highams (11)
Marish Primary School, Slough

Petrified

Petrified is the colour of white like snow
It tastes horrific like you just ate rancid food
It smells like damp wood in a slippery, slimy swamp
It looks like you in a frozen ice block
It sounds like a continuous buzzing noise
It feels like you are in your own little world with nobody beside you.

Tevin Johnson (10)
Marish Primary School, Slough

Video Games

I am addicted to video games
Like a wasp is attracted to sweetness
Like children are inspired by their favourite football player
Like fleas are attracted to dirty hair.

I am addicted to video games
How about you, are you addicted to video games?
Have you ever been on an aeroplane?

Shai Bane (10)
Marish Primary School, Slough

Wasp Horror

I am terrified by wasps
Like the burning sun is afraid of the shining moon
Like a worm is shocked by a swooping eagle
Like chocolate ice cream is nervous of sporty kids
Like a white furry cat is horrified of a patchy dog
Like a snail is anxious of an adult's foot
I'm terrified by wasps.

Lucy Robbins (10)
Marish Primary School, Slough

Happy

Happy is blue like the sky
It tastes like sugar
It smells like roses
It looks like friends playing together
It sounds like laughter
It feels like your tummy is jumping up and down.

Levi Stroud (10)
Marish Primary School, Slough

My Delights

I am inspired by strawberry ice cream
Like the sun is loved by children
Like the fish are obsessed by the sea
Like a pen is attached to paper
Like a football is desperate for a goal
Like the moon is incomplete without stars
I am inspired by strawberry ice cream!

Vrinda Kanani (11)
Marish Primary School, Slough

My Shoes

My shoes are special to me
My shoes are everything to me
My shoes are precious to me
My shoes always come with me
My shoes are always there for me
My shoes always travel with me.

Jordan Keeley (10)
Marish Primary School, Slough

Joyful

Joyful is pink like roses
It tastes like Turkish Delight
It smells like fresh air
It looks like a bunch of strawberries
It sounds like birds singing
It feels like butterflies flying in your tummy.

Tilly Burden (11)
Marish Primary School, Slough

Fright

Fright comes in all shapes and sizes
Slithery green or lazy or keen
It tastes rough and bumpy
But smells utterly empty
It looks . . . then strikes
But sounds frightfully light
It feels scaly
But hunts daily
It's a snake
Hiss!

Qasim Durrani (10)
Marish Primary School, Slough

Gym

I am attracted to gymnastics
Like the 60s and a dime
Like a monkey and banana
And a swimmer and a pool
Like a sock with cheese
Like a tractor and a farm
And that's you and me.

Rachel Hood (10)
Marish Primary School, Slough

Sinister Sadness

Sadness is grey like a rainy day
Sadness tastes like mouldy hay
Sadness looks like a dead rat
Sadness smells like a damp cat
Sadness sounds like galloping horses
Sadness feels like eating ten courses.

Emma Hughes (10)
Marish Primary School, Slough

Wonders Of Laughter

Laughter is the colour of the sparkling glimmering rainbow
It tastes of bright bursting Smarties
It smells of pretty scented flowers
It looks like a beautiful butterfly
It sounds like a group of cats fighting
It feels tingly and warm
It is filled with love.

Hannah Nicholls (10)
Marish Primary School, Slough

Love

Love is red like a balloon sailing towards the sky
It tastes like a roast dinner on a Saturday afternoon
It smells like melted chocolate on cold strawberries
It looks like your first cuddly bear you got when you were two
It sounds like your first kiss on a moonlit night
It feels warm and cuddly like your blanket you cuddle up in every night.

Charles O'Neill (10)
Marish Primary School, Slough

Joyfulness

Joy is yellow like blooming daffodils
It tastes like hot custard on cold, cold nights
It smells like a bowl of fruit shining in the sun
It sounds like people crushing the yellow autumn leaves.

Ghadiyah Mobashir (10)
Marish Primary School, Slough

Terriphobia

A pencil is terrified of an erasing rubber
Like the sun is envied by the moon
Like a nail is horrified of a smashing hammer
Like a person is afraid of a long-legged tarantula
Like a dog is anxious about getting put into a deep sleep
Like a piece of paper is nervous about getting ripped
A pencil is terrified of an erasing rubber.

Elliott Ogbebor (10)
Marish Primary School, Slough

Fear

Fear is black like thundery clouds
It tastes like cold rice pudding
It smells like the smoke of the night sky
It looks like you're in a misty alleyway
It sounds like screeching of a blackboard
It feels like looking down from the top of a mountain.

Ryan Gulliford (11)
Marish Primary School, Slough

I Like

I am inspired by video games
Like paper is addicted to a pen
Like children are attracted to sugar
Like a lid is attached to a bottle
Like a child glued to a Game Boy.

Shabazz Siddiq (10)
Marish Primary School, Slough

Happiness

Happiness, happiness
Happiness everywhere
The colour of happiness is yellow
And it smells like a pure open meadow
Happiness, happiness
Happiness everywhere
It sounds so wonderful to hear about
And feels so good to smile about
Happiness, happiness
Happiness everywhere
All you need is happiness
To exchange anger into calmness.

Srinithiy Aravinthanathan (10)
Marish Primary School, Slough

Amusement

I am amused by laughter
Like a clown in a crowd
Like a dog chasing sheep into their pen
Like a farmer grabbing ostrich eggs
Like a man playing with his newborn son
Like a roadrunner sprinting away from a coyote
I am amused by laughter.

Charlie Hood (10)
Marish Primary School, Slough

My Pencil Case

My pencil case is perfect, as perfect as can be
Whenever I am looking down, it's always there for me
Especially when I'm getting bored, it always cheers me up
Then one day it lost me, I didn't know what to do
The next day this kind girl came to me
And she said, 'I have a surprise for you.'
She found my pencil case
My pencil case is perfect, as perfect as can be.

Jasveet Heer (10)
Marish Primary School, Slough

The Boot

I am inspired by football
Like my boot willing to kick a football
Like the net is attached to the goalkeeper's gloves
As he tried to save the shot
Like my studs inspired by the muddy grass
Like a swimming pool attracted to the people as they jump in
Like bees hypnotised by honey
And I always will be.

Bradley Thorpe (10)
Marish Primary School, Slough

Loudly

Loudly the giant stomps through the cold air
Loudly the thunder crashes in the sky
Loudly the fireworks explode up high
Loudly the cars drive on the motorway
Loudly the church bells ring in the tower
Loudly the jets fly in the air
But loudest of all are the children shouting.

Tara Spargo (8)
Moorlands Primary School, Reading

Brightly

Brightly the light bulb is shining
Brightly the spotlights glimmer
Brightly the moon is gleaming
Brightly the stars shimmer.

Brightly the fireworks glow
Brightly the sun shines
Brightly the rainbow is shiny
Brightly the colour yellow brightens the day.

Taylor Miles (8)
Moorlands Primary School, Reading

Loudly

Loudly the thunder crashes in the sky
Loudly the babies rattle, rattling all the time
Loudly the rain pitter-patters on the concrete
Loudly the wind whooshing through the window
Loudly the children shouting, making a noise
Loudly a baby crying for her food
Loudly cymbals crashing, making a noise
Drums drumming in the band.

Gemma Driver (9)
Moorlands Primary School, Reading

Swiftly

Swiftly the tornado travels across the sea
Swiftly the spider catches a flea
Swiftly the person hurries to town
Swiftly the hamster scurries around.

Swiftly the tiger fed on its prey
Swiftly the rocket sped far away
Swiftly the swift flew like a kite
But swiftest of all is the speed of light.

Lekan Olasina (8)
Moorlands Primary School, Reading

Bright

Brightly the fireworks pop in the window
Brightly the fire crackles in the posh house
Brightly the time vortex spins in the dark
Brightly the whiteboard glitters in the classroom
Brightly the sun burns in the sky
Brightly the clouds shimmer in the sky
Brightly the moon turns in the black sky.

Emma Harris (8)
Moorlands Primary School, Reading

Brightly

Brightly candles shine like lava spilling from a volcano
Brightly a torch shines like a spotlight
Brightly stars shine in the darkness
Brightly the sun shines in the summer
Brightly fireworks vanish into thin air
Brightly the moon gleams at night-time.

Owen Gould (8)
Moorlands Primary School, Reading

Brightly

Brightly the small torch glowed in the dark forest
Brightly the mutant lava burnt my head
Brightly the burning fire demolished the building
Brightly the lamp post gleamed over me
Brightly the stars beamed on the Earth
Brightly the white candle toppled on the carpet.

Jack Chester (8)
Moorlands Primary School, Reading

Brightly

Brightly the fireworks popped in the distance
Brightly the torch flashed in the air
Brightly the glowsticks shine in the dark
Brightly the sun glowed in the blue sky
Brightly the light bulbs smashed in the house
Brightly the flashlights flickered on the car
Brightly the lamps went all crazy on the tree branches
Brightly the candles melted in the church.

Natasha Hallett (9)
Moorlands Primary School, Reading

Brightly

Brightly a firework falls over land
Brightly the trophy sparkles on the dull floor
Brightly the moon reflects on the lake
Brightly the stars shone on the rooftops
Brightly the lights glow along the house
Brightly the sun lights up the sky.

Shannon Townley-Taylor (8)
Moorlands Primary School, Reading

Brightly

Brightly the sun glows in the sky
Brightly the lava flows in the volcano
Brightly the fire spits on the logs
Brightly the Bunsen burner burns in the lab
Brightly the lights heat up on the roof.

Thomas Savin (8)
Moorlands Primary School, Reading

Loudly

Loudly the thunder bangs in the sky
Loudly the church bells ring in the church
Loudly the football fans cheer for their team
Loudly the rocket blasts into space.

Loudly the cymbals clash in the band
Loudly the racing cars roar in the Grand Prix
Loudly the fireworks explode in the air
Loudly the drum beats in time.

Charly Fox (8)
Moorlands Primary School, Reading

Brightly

Brightly the torch shines up the garden path
Brightly the fire cracks up the wall
Brightly the fireworks popping in the sky
Brightly the glowsticks wave in people's hands
Brightly the sun shimmers in the summer sky
Brightly the stars twinkle in the night sky
Brightly the lava crackles up the wall.

Chloe Clifford (8)
Moorlands Primary School, Reading

Brightly

Brightly the ice cube glows in the darkness
Brightly the moon shines in the dusky sky
Brightly the stars glitter in the darkness
Brightly the sun gleams in the fiery water
Brightly the metal tins shine in the sky above.

Amber Willis (8)
Moorlands Primary School, Reading

The Door

(Based on 'The Door' by Miroslav Holub)

Go and open the door
Maybe there's a dark chocolate cake on a table
An Indian waving a flag, a table with some flowers in a vase
Or a river with a red and white fish in it.

Go and open the door
Maybe outside there's a pirate with a dagger waving it around
A chocolate world full of chocolate
Or a plasma TV with your favourite TV programme
A distant island with lots of trees
Or a pile of chewy sour sweets.

Go and open the door
Maybe outside there's a wobbling eyeball on the floor
Or a magic carpet ready to fly away.

Ben Gowers (8)
Moorlands Primary School, Reading

The Door

(Based on 'The Door' by Miroslav Holub)

Go and open the door
Maybe outside there's a beautiful young girl
A red cosy sofa with fluffy pillows and a shiny grey TV.

Go and open the door
Maybe outside there's a silver water dispenser fridge
A laptop with every game on it, a black dog with brown on its chest.

Go and open the door
Maybe outside there's a pink phone
Waiting for me to ring my friends
A bedroom waiting for me to sleep in
A cat that is black and white.

Chloe Gunn (8)
Moorlands Primary School, Reading

The Door

(Based on 'The Door' by Miroslav Holub)

Go and open the door
Maybe outside there's a blue and red sofa
A golden but dirty tree
A beach covered in sand and salty sea
And a herd of vampires trying to look for human blood.

Go and open the door
Maybe there's an ice cream bowl
Longing for someone to eat it
A firework going off into colours
Maybe New York's out there with Doctor Who
A smelly dead fish smelling like an ogre
A gleaming red water bottle reflecting off the sun.

Go and open the door
Maybe there's an imaginary world of lots of chocolate
And a very, very sad girl crying her eyes out.

Zoë Evans (8)
Moorlands Primary School, Reading

Loudly

Loudly the drum goes *boom, boom, boom*
Loudly the thunderstorm goes *bang, boom, bang*
Loudly you can hear the building site from miles going *crash,*
bang, crash
Loudly the rocket goes *zoom* as it blasted out into space
Loudly the baby cries in the night, *wah, wah, wah*
Loudly the noisy road goes *zoom, zoom, zoom*
Loudly the cymbals make music, *crash, crash, bang, whiz.*

Molly Chandler (9)
Moorlands Primary School, Reading

The Door

(Based on 'The Door' by Miroslav Holub)

Go and open the door
Maybe there is a big cream chocolate cake
A chocolate world and a chocolate fountain.

Go and open the door
Maybe there is lots of puppies and kittens
Or a big party or a coffin.

Go and open the door
Maybe there's a disco ball
A big garden or a club.

Go and open the door
Maybe there are people singing or people dancing
A golden table with a bunch of flowers in a pot.

Go and open the door
Maybe there is a comfy chair with a fluffy cushion on it
Or another red door.

Deven King (8)
Moorlands Primary School, Reading

The Door

(Based on 'The Door' by Miroslav Holub)

Go and open the door
Maybe outside there's an old rusty telephone
A pile of creamy chocolate
A big scary statue or a sandy seaside.

Go and open the door
Maybe there's a pretty water fountain
Maybe you'll see a slimy frog having a walk
A car going 100mph or a big fluffy dog.

Go and open the door
Even if there's nothing
Go and open the door.

Lydia Giles (9)
Moorlands Primary School, Reading

Go And Open The Door

(Based on 'The Door' by Miroslav Holub)

Go and open the door
Maybe outside there's cities dancing
Aliens invading, jungle roaring.

Go and open the door
Maybe there's a haunted house scaring you
A boat sailing out to sea
Maybe there's a king's castle waiting for me.

Go and open the door
Maybe there's dog barking
Cats scratching, lions biting.

Go and open the door
Maybe there's people eating
Aunties yelling, mums working.

Even if there's nothing there
Go and open the door.

Dion Holley (8)
Moorlands Primary School, Reading

Swiftly

Swiftly the rocket blasts into space
Swiftly the supersonic jet speeds rapidly
Swiftly the tornado travels over the sea
Swiftly the hot-air balloon glides over the town.

Swiftly the bat flies into the cave
Swiftly the cheetah runs through the African plains
Swiftly the thief runs out of the shop
But the swiftest of all, the speed of light.

Gautham Senthilnathan (8)
Moorlands Primary School, Reading

Silently

Silently the swan floats on the cold blue water
Silently the grass sways to the breeze
Silently the wind blows through the cornfield
Silently the tree grows towards the sky.

Silently the mouse creeps through the leaves
Silently the fish glides slowly under the waves
Silently the star shoots across the sky
Silently the ant crawls under the ground.

Amy Thatcher (8)
Moorlands Primary School, Reading

Brightly

Brightly the moon glows in the night
Brightly a diamond glistening in the light
Brightly the stars twinkle in the sky
Brightly a rainbow so colourful and high.

Brightly the lightning flashes so quick
Brightly a wand sparkles in a flick
Brightly the sun, so big and round
But brightest of all, a fire on the ground.

Rachel Peasley (8)
Moorlands Primary School, Reading

Swiftly

Swiftly the cat pounces at its prey
Swiftly the hamster scurries away
swiftly the rocket lifts off up into space
Swiftly the swift flies brightly through the air.

Swiftly the motorbike speeds down the motorway
Swiftly the supersonic jet takes off
Swiftly the children run down the stairs at break
But swiftest of all is the speed of *light*.

Max Edinborough (8)
Moorlands Primary School, Reading

How Many?

How many stars are in the sky
Shining brightly through the night?
How many stars are in the sky
Showing off in such bright light?

How many strands of hair are there
On every animal with hair?
How many strands of hair are there
And are they very fair?

How many grains of sand are there
Washing through the gentle waves?
How many grains of sand are there?
Counting them would take days!

Jemima Bentley (10)
Oaklands Junior School, Crowthorne

Mountain Tops

Mountains high
You'd have to fly
Snow on the top and loads of frost
Mountains so big
Everything looks like toys
And I can see young funny boys
Sheep on it climbing as well
I got a towel out because I am cold
I go back to the lodge and watch TV
And listen to the melody.

Sophie Bowman (10)
Oaklands Junior School, Crowthorne

Hiawatha

(With apologies to H W Longfellow)

'Give me of your fur, O Tiger
Of your rich fur, O Tiger
Living in the depths of Siberia
Majestic and tall in the plain
I, a fur coat will fashion me
Fashion a heavy coat for winter
To keep me warm in the depths and heart of winter
Lay aside your orange cloak, O Tiger
Lay aside your orange fur cloak
For the hot season is coming
And the sun's rays are warm and welcoming
And you need no orange fur cloak!'
Thus aloud cried Hiawatha.

And the Tiger with all its might
Shivered in the breeze of dawn
Saying with a quiver of dread,
'Take my fur, O Hiawatha.'
With his knife the Tiger he skinned
Just beneath the legs
Just above the tail he cut it
All over the body from tail to belly
Bare he left the Tiger's cold torso
With a wooden sled he dragged it
Stripped it from the body cleanly.

Felicity Boss (10)
Oaklands Junior School, Crowthorne

Seasons

The bare trees, the windy days
The cold nights, the snow that lays
The crunching of footsteps in the snow
The calm icy rivers cease to flow
Snowflakes falling gently to the ground
Everyone knows winter's around.

Spring is here, everyone cheer
The snow has gone, here comes the sun
It might be cold, as I've been told
But the flowers are out
Everyone shout, it's spring!

All the trees are tall and green
It's summertime, so don't be mean
Put on your sunglasses and have a ball
'Cause summer's here but it's almost fall
Go to the beach, get out in the sun
Summer's here and it's so much fun!

All the leaves are falling down
They soon begin to turn red and brown
There might even be a little sun
So we can try to have some fun
The harvest festival is coming to town
Let's celebrate 'cause autumn's around!

Asha Birly (10)
Oaklands Junior School, Crowthorne

The Bird Of The Night

Swooping down upon the Earth
Gliding, soaring gracefully
Even for all it's worth
It never stops amazing me.

As I sit under a lonely tree
Calling for the stars
Only some come to me
Whenever I may call.

But now my work is almost done
As the night sky fills
But as the darkness runs from the sun
My work has just begun.

Alex Wilson (11)
Oaklands Junior School, Crowthorne

The Lion

Mighty lion I am
A strong powerful animal
I am stronger than man
So don't challenge me.

The proud and elegant lion I am
An animal can challenge me
I'm not afraid
But I wouldn't.

Pretty and beautiful lion I am
You'll risk your life
If you challenge me
Mighty lion I am.

Laura Martin (10)
Oaklands Junior School, Crowthorne

Chocolate

Chocolate here, chocolate there
Chocolate everywhere
Soft or crunchy
Smooth or creamy
What a joy
What a delight
Chocolate that I can have every night
White and brown and black all around
Tastes so sweet
Tastes so nice
I just want to take a big old bite.

Abbie Butler (10)
Oaklands Junior School, Crowthorne

Magic

Magic
It's another world
Sometimes it can be heard
You can see the fairies in the sky
Now that's quite high
In books
Fairies hid in nooks
You see
Wish it could be . . .
Magic!

Sophie Harding (8)
Oaklands Junior School, Crowthorne

Think . . .

Sometimes I wonder what to think about
It makes me think quite hard
So here I sit with a head full of nought
And I come up with an idea.

The idea I thought, I think will really work
So here it is with a little twist
Oh no, I forgot what it was
Think, think, think . . .

Lyle Dalgleish (10)
Oaklands Junior School, Crowthorne

Music

Music, music, I love the sound
Makes me want to howl like a hound
Music, music, makes me move
I love to do the groovy groove
Music, music, wherever it is
Makes want to sing like this,
'La, la, la, la, la!'

Rosie Stevens (10)
Oaklands Junior School, Crowthorne

I Love Horses

My horse is brown with rough hair
My horse's legs are powerful like a racing car
My horse's eyes are big and bold
My horse's nose is as cold as ice
My horse's mouth is as wet as water . . .

Holly Cook (10)
Oaklands Junior School, Crowthorne

Happiness

Happiness sounds like I'm laughing to myself
Happiness smells like bluebells in the forest
Happiness tastes like sweets
Happiness looks like butterflies flapping in the sky
Happiness feels like ice cream
Happiness reminds me of going on holiday.

Jordan Bird (7)
Rangefield Primary School, Bromley

Happiness

Happiness sounds like people laughing off their fun
Happiness smells wonderful
Happiness tastes like sweets
Happiness feels like softness
Happiness reminds me of my daddy.

Camila Rocha (7)
Rangefield Primary School, Bromley

Love

Love sounds like angels singing in the air
Love tastes like air when your lips are dry
Love smells like two people in love forever
Love looks like two people together forever
Love feels like an emotion when you like somebody.

Owen Amenze (7)
Rangefield Primary School, Bromley

Happiness

Happiness is fun
Happiness is beautiful
Happiness is true
Happiness is when children are laughing
Happiness smells like the sea waving in the wind.

Isabel Paulin (7)
Rangefield Primary School, Bromley

Sadness

Sadness sounds like somebody crying when they have no friends
It tastes like when you're lonely
It smells like bad pancakes
Sadness reminds me of telling the teacher.

Ayten Azimkar (7)
Rangefield Primary School, Bromley

Heat

I've got a sunhat
Yellow, green and blue
I drew the sunhat
And the sunhat drew you
Sunhats are useful for all types of weather
Sunhats are used to having fun
Strong glue is used for sticking down feathers
That is the end of this poem
I can say the job is well done.

Elizabeth Rillie (10)
St Michael's Easthampstead CE School, Bracknell

If It Weren't For School

If it weren't for school,
I could run and run and run about
And play on the computer till my eyes popped out
Or sometimes I might play a game
Or run around and be a pain
But if I didn't want to do them
I'd play around or write with a pen.
I'd read lots and lots and lots of books
Instead of hanging coats on hooks
And then I'd play my violin
And make a completely awful din
Until my quiet mum would say,
Go out to find bugs for the rest of the day!

Joanna Cook (9)
St Michael's Easthampstead CE School, Bracknell

Aliens

Aliens think they are cool
Aliens have taken over the school
Aliens don't have a vest
Aliens don't have any rest
Aliens fly in space
Aliens have a horrible face
Aliens have taken my brother
Aliens have taken my mother
Aliens are trying to take over the human race
But first I must tie my lace
Humans also fight and aliens have a flight
Back to Pluto where it's not in sight.

Sudarshan Gurumoorthy (9)
St Michael's Easthampstead CE School, Bracknell

The Rainbow

S himmering past
U p in the air
M aking joyful pathways
M oss is green, plants are cheery
E aster's left behind, so's spring
R ainbows sway and dance

F ollow them quick
U p in the air
N ever stopping

T wirling around
I nto a land
M ade beautiful
E xcited that summer's here!

Zoë Green (9)
St Michael's Easthampstead CE School, Bracknell

September

S is for Susie, my nickname
E is an excellent birthday month
P is for parties on the 11th
T is for my friend Tanvi
E is for eating party food
M is for making decorations
B is for being the party queen
E is for enjoying party time
R is for racing a party game.

Susanna Rillie (9)
St Michael's Easthampstead CE School, Bracknell

Autumn

The wind in my hair
But the trees look so bare
That's a sign of autumn.

The bound of a dog
I can't see through the fog
That's another sign of autumn.

The smell of apple pie
Hallowe'en stuff to buy . . .
Autumn is here.

Natalie Miles (10)
St Michael's Easthampstead CE School, Bracknell

Summer

Apples falling
My friends yawning
Hot people on the beach
Can you see Mrs Leach?
She's in the van
Reading a plan
To mend a fan
From Japan.

Katherine Simpson (9)
St Michael's Easthampstead CE School, Bracknell

Dreams

Dreams can be good and bad
Dreams can be happy and sad
Dream on, go on dream
I love to dream I do, I do, I do
No one can stop dreaming
Not even me
Stop dreaming, stop
No one can stop me from dreaming, no one
Oh no, not bad dreams, no, no
Too bad, no more dreaming for me.

Lauren Charlton (8)
St Michael's Easthampstead CE School, Bracknell

Snow Tiger

Mine is the fur so soft and fluffy
In cold snow-like air
That makes me scruffy.

Mine are the eyes that glow in the dark
As blue as sapphires
That make my mark.

Mine is the growl that rumbles through the trees
Across the land
Leaves blow in the breeze.

Frances Senn (9)
The Russell School, Richmond

Great White Shark

Mine are the jaws
That scare people away
In my watery lair
Mine is the prey.

Mine is the nose
That breathes with fear
When death is close
Mine is the ear.

Mine are the teeth
The divers trade
Mine are the teeth
I am afraid.

Hussain Merchant (9)
The Russell School, Richmond

Snake

Mine are the eyes
That stop my prey
In the savannah heat
Day by day.

Mine is the tongue
That's shaped like a fork.
Quivering in cool night air
With my single tail I walk.

Mine is the skin
The huntsmen collect;
Patterns so attractive
They find it hard to select.

Naomi Edwards (9)
The Russell School, Richmond

Stockholm

I step outside, the wind runs up to me
Kicks me and steals my hat
I walk past the picturesque houses
As they stand tall in front of me.

I see the sun staring thoughtfully at Gamla Stan
The old part of town
Where handmade paper, ceramics and glittering crystals
Sit in glass cases waiting to be sold.

The clouds float lazily over Stockholm
Looking down from the bridge
I see the water as blue as a sapphire.

I walk up the elongated staircase
Longing to get to the top of the Kaknas Tower
From the 508 foot high platform
I see the Royal Palace, home to Sweden's monarchs
Grinning in the sunshine.

As I walk home the wind calls to me
Asking me to come over
He hums a little tune
And returns my hat.

Gabriel Alveteg (10)
The Russell School, Richmond

Berlin

I see the tall skyscrapers staring in my eye
The parliament building seeking for some shade
The Brandenburg Gate standing proudly in the light
A galloping horse with a statue wobbling around the corner
The tomb of the Duke of Brunswick looking down
With the cold and silver colours shining in the twilight
Buses, cars and trains driving round to see all the places and more.

Joseph Ochieng (10)
The Russell School, Richmond

Istanbul

The Blue Mosque stands tall as its blue tiles sparkle
Cars spring round shouting at each other
The St Sophia Museum jumps high in the sky
Rugs in shops float in the wind
And the spices of the Spice Market dance around
The Topkapi Palace pays tribute to the emperor
Fishermen fish in the waters of the Black Sea
That gets angry at humans who jump in.

The Grand Bazzar is always crowded
The Golden Horn sways with glittering ripples
The streets are crowded with hundreds, no thousands of humans
Istanbul is a lovely place to be.

Owain Strassburg (10)
The Russell School, Richmond

Vienna

I arrive in Vienna, the sun smiling and the sky bright blue
The streets, congested like a shopping mall
Wind around like the roots of a tree
St Stephen's Cathedral looms over me as I pass
And the Grand State Opera House sings like a choir
I walk along the Danube watching speedboats zip by
A wonderful blinding view under the gleaming summer sky
The National Theatre stands tall with pride
And from Maria Hilferstrasse wafts a wonderful smell of cakes
The streets are now empty, the sun has gone to bed
The stars are now glimmering in the midnight sky
So that's the great Vienna with all its wonderful views
And its delicious Sachertorte which never makes you blue.

Danny Knight (11)
The Russell School, Richmond

Rome

I am arriving in Rome
I feel the cold air rushing past me
I can hear the Colosseum roaring with madness
The hotel shining like diamonds welcoming me to their warm rooms
Looking at this Eternal City, I'm going to see the sights
The Trevi Fountain in the distance
I see people throwing coins, hoping they will come back to Rome
Into St Peter's I walk and look at the fabulous paintings
And ecclesiastical treasures
The sun smiling at me and the Spanish steps dancing in front of me
It is lovely in Rome
I smell the delicious pizza that I will never forget
I leave Rome but know I will never forget this
Extraordinary city until next time . . .

Rana El-Hoshi (11)
The Russell School, Richmond

My Enchanting But Terrifying Journey

As I skip along the smooth path
The tropical, enchanting forest whispers its welcome to me
A spectacular scarlet orchid blossoms
As shafts of sun fill it with beauty
The pollen from the flowers fills my nose with enticing scent
As the lush green trees shade me from danger.

As I trudge through the soggy earth
The terrifying forest drones, advising me to stop and turn back
The damp rotten smell hurts my nose
The fungi start to crawl beneath my feet
The poisonous odour makes me feel dizzy
As the grey clouds appear up above.

Sophie Smith (10)
The Russell School, Richmond

Copenhagen

The magical oldest kingdom still stands today
Cars cough and choke past me
The sun gazed down at me
While tall buildings surround me
Colourful boats sway gently in the water.

The Little Mermaid's eyes light up the statue
As a shiver travels up my spine
Delicious smells waft out of the restaurants pulling me in
Watch the Changing of the Guard at Amalienborg Palace
Finally, fall into Stoget's beautiful shops
Which jump out asking you to buy their wares
Copenhagen is a lovely place to be in.

Ella Strutt (10)
The Russell School, Richmond

Milan

The Gothic cathedral, staring down at me like an angry man
The colours and fabrics of the fashion models
Are shimmering in the sun
The Sforzesco castle with its towers pointing to the sky
The restaurants calling me in with their delicious smell
The Duomo's carvings are as neat as a man in a suit
La Scala relaxes me with its musical voice
Milan - an exciting place to see!

Hayleigh Gallimore (10)
The Russell School, Richmond

Copenhagen

The old kingdom still standing today
The trees in the park sway, sway, sway
The Little Mermaid winking at me
The sun sizzling down on the sea.

The cars cough and beep
People on colourful boats chat and shout
Walking on the streets past full packed restaurants
Smelling the traditional meal, roast pork with red cabbage.

Travelling on foot
Watching the changing of the guards at Amalienborg Palace
Enjoy the night life
Jazz clubs and night clubs, music so loud you dance all night
Copenhagen is a wonderful place to be!

Tara Kermani (11)
The Russell School, Richmond

Istanbul

The Blue Mosque stands proudly as its blue tiles glitter in the sun
The amazing St Sophia Museum stands tall
The Black Sea burns the swimmers jumping in
Taxis queue on the crowded street as cars honk their horns.

The smell of the spices floats around the Spice Mark
As tourists come strolling in
The store holders' shouts can be heard from the Grand Bazaar
The smell of seafood fills the air
As the fishermen come back from their hard day's work.

Matthew Bartholomew (10)
The Russell School, Richmond

My Autumn Walk

As the sun awakes my alarm clock rings
I am off for an autumn walk
I look up into the foggy sky
I see a pale white sun rising above gleaming golden trees
The conkers look out of their lime-green shells
Like squinting eyes from underneath the sodden brown leaves
When I walk past the allotment
I see huge orange pumpkins with bendy green stalks
I trudge home and think how nice it has been
And of all the drawings I will be doing from the images in my head.

Daniel De Rozairo (8)
The Russell School, Richmond

Brussels

Sweet bread and Belgian chocolate, French fries are the best
Pretty paintings just like Van Gogh's
The food in the restaurants is better than junk food
The doors on the buildings just sneezed open in front of me
And gave me a fright
The chocolate in this country is so nice, I wouldn't even get full
The sweet bread is so sweet I'll probably have a sweet tooth tomorrow
I'll always remember the sweet bread in Brussels.

Hanicka Hall-Howitt (10)
The Russell School, Richmond

Vienna

The Schonbrunn Palace entices me into its fairyland castle
The doors sneeze open, swarms of people queue in the corridors
And snake into the exhibition
Taxis jump along the road as I look up in the sky
The sun smiles at me, what's happening?
Inside, it's amazing, like a dream
I will never forget this extraordinary palace in Vienna.

Ashleigh Denney (10)
The Russell School, Richmond

Penguin

Mine is the beak
That catches the eye
Mothers leave their young
And say goodbye.

Mine is the honk
That makes people laugh
In the big wide sea
I like to bath.

Mine are the feet
Waddling along
Sliding on ice
Honking my song.

Kaja Sillett (9)
The Russell School, Richmond

Bear

Mine are the eyes
That always shine
In my mountain den
Mine is the whine.

Mine are the claws
That rip and pierce
When I stalk my prey
My growl is fierce.

Mine are the teeth
That chatter in fear
I am afraid
The huntsmen are here.

Wilhelm Johannis (9)
The Russell School, Richmond

Wolf

Mine is the howl
That shivers you down
In the woods alone
You run back to town.

Mine are the eyes
That glow in the dark
Stalking my prey
I make my mark.

Mine is the fur
That blends me in
Staying in the shadows
I commit my sin.

Amelia McLay (9)
The Russell School, Richmond

Snake

Mine is the venom
From the spit of my mouth
It's an easy kill
Down the jungle in the south.

Mine is the body
Camouflaged in the light
With greeny-yellow skin
It's too bright.

Mine is the skin
From my body I shed
Sometimes it hurts
And people think I'm dead.

Sam El-Hadidy (9)
The Russell School, Richmond

Polar Bear

Mine are the claws
That scrape the ice
In the cold Arctic snow
Mine is the slice.

Mine is the snow
That breaks my world
When the snow falls
My claws are unfurled.

Mine are the eyes
That sparkle in the light
In the cold sky
Mine is the white.

Anil Gizli (9)
The Russell School, Richmond

Polar Bear

Mine is the pure white
That stops the heart
But snow comes crashing
My world falls apart.

Mine is the ample
Bulk that kills
I am a carnivore
And my lair chills.

Mine is the growl
That echoes on the ice
In the snowy cold
You will pay the price.

Scarlett Cawley (10)
The Russell School, Richmond

Streets

Streets at day, streets at night
There are different kinds of sights
Streets in snow, streets in rain
Even in a hurricane.

Most of all there is one more
Hailstones are the worst
I am not really sure
But I think there is just one more.

Francesca Woolf (7)
The Russell School, Richmond

Autumn Sights

Cold misty day outside
Crunch, crunch, crunch!
Leaves are crispy and crunchy
Cold and foggy
Shiny freezing conkers and chestnuts
Spiders' webs shine like little buttons
On a necklace when it rains.

Alexander Gancitano (8)
The Russell School, Richmond

Paris

The Eiffel Tower standing tall
Taxis coughing around the town
Motorbikes rattling through the traffic lights
Lorries roaring through the daylight
The long glimmering limos stretching down the street
The smell of magnificent food fading through the street
Kids jumping up and down, waiting for their creations
Before they start to frown.

Tom Kipps (10)
The Russell School, Richmond

Venice

Venice, known for the Grand Canal
That flows round corners like a fish in the sea
Try having a cup of coffee in St Mark's Square.

The Doges Palace, tall and beautiful
With shiny walls of mirrors and gleaming paintings
The light of the Rialto Bridge winking at me in the moonlight.

Imagine having seafood with wine in a beautiful restaurant
Take a motorboat ride from the Bay of Venice to the open lagoon
I will always remember Venice!

Melissa Jassar (10)
The Russell School, Richmond

A Walk In Autumn

Straight away early in the morning
I stepped outside for a walk
Mist was like smoke on a fire
Spiders' webs covered in dew looked like crystal necklaces
Leaves were all on the ground ready to be crunched by my feet
I saw a bunch of hedgehogs trying to stay warm
Taking my scarf off I put it on their crunchy spiky backs
Conkers were scattered around the floor, cold as snow itself
But that's what it's like in autumn.

Eleanor McLay (8)
The Russell School, Richmond

My Walk Outside

As I walk through a misty and cold grass
I see leaves fall off trees
I hear trees blow in the cold, cold weather
I see the nice shiny conkers fall off the trees
My fingers get numb, I can't feel them
I walk through a foggy lane
People walk past me, I get colder and colder
I feel goosebumps go up and down my body as I walk faster
I feel the wind blow across my face
Then I walk and I feel the cold breeze
My feet are as cold as ice.

Ria Ramnauth (9)
The Russell School, Richmond

My Walk In Autumn

When I look out of my window I see that Jack Frost has been,
It is shiny and shimmery I am so glad to see.
When I walk down the street all the leaves have fallen at my feet,
Colours so tender and sweet.
When I go down the alleyway I see the mist on the trees
With the leaves all falling on me.
When I am nearly at school I see a little squirrel hibernating.
At school I say goodbye,
But I will come back to say goodnight.

Jemma Thorne (8)
The Russell School, Richmond

The Riverbank

The river is overflowing
The sea is going from the river
The river is not overflowing, yay, yay
The sea is calm hooray, hooray today.

The riverbank is calm over here hooray
Shall we have a picnic with honey from the bee?
Shall we have a picnic with milk from the butterflies?
What shall we do on a wonderful day like this?

The riverbank is overflowing
The picnic is destroyed, how but argh
Even now the river is calm, let's go for a swim
Come on, come on, it's fun, come on.

Let's get an ice cream, let's, let's, let's
Ice cream is cold as cold as can be
Ow, let's get one ice cream to share
Our tongues get stuck on a really cold ice cream.

Hannah Strassburg (7)
The Russell School, Richmond

Autumn Stroll

Conkers falling from the tree
I see the dew on the shiny wet grass
I kick the leaves on the rough pavement
But the spooky mist is so foggy I can barely see
I see the animals hibernate and realise it's autumn
I think how fast the time has gone from spring to summer to autumn
I can't believe it's gone so quickly
Soon it will be winter!

Finn Stammers (8)
The Russell School, Richmond

Autumn, Winter

Autumn, winter, the misty fog was out
Opening my window I smell the fresh air
Going downstairs I put my wellies on
Then run outside and see the beautiful sunshine
All the conkers peeping out of the leaves
The spider's web filled with dew like a diamond necklace
Now I am out here it seems so strange
I smell again to check, same smell.

Paige Fisher (8)
The Russell School, Richmond

The Leaves

Autumn is the time when the leaves fall off the trees
Crackle, crackle, crackle
The leaves turn beautiful colours like browns and reds
Crackle, crackle, crackle
I love walking through the forest and collecting conkers
Watching them come down in their spiky shells
Crackle, crackle, crackle!

Katya Camyab (8)
The Russell School, Richmond

About Autumn

The conkers are peeking through the colourful leaves
The floor is more crunchy than you have ever seen
It's misty on the ground, it's misty in the air
The dew comes out in the soft, soft grass
I'm cold in the morning so I stay home today
The plants die out when the mist is around.

Nina Van Cranenburgh (8)
The Russell School, Richmond

Colours Under The Sea

Under the sea there are magical fish
Some of all sizes and colours
Some that live right at the bottom
Some that live with others.

Under the sea there are wonderful sights
Like the colours of the coral
With all the wonderful rainbow fish
Beauty is the sea's moral.

Isabella Endacott (8)
The Russell School, Richmond

Fox's Howl

A fox's howl, a howl to break the silence of the night
A howl like a scowl of doom
A shadow of a black fox's head
A mark of death.

David Bustos (7)
The Russell School, Richmond

Orange

Orange like lava pouring down a volcano
Orange like a fox running off in the night
Orange like fire coming out of a dragon's mouth
Orange like a ginger cat on the prowl.

Luke Bartholomew (7)
The Russell School, Richmond

My Sister Kitty

My sister is called Kitty
And she is so pretty
She cries a lot
And smiles when she's not.

She likes to pull my hair
And I don't even care
Her favourite toy is a drumstick
And she likes to lick it.

She laughs so much
When you touch
Her chubby cheek
Any day of the week.

Louie Bevins-Martin (7)
The Russell School, Richmond

Peace

People screaming
Looking for safety

Each and all
Worried and scared

After the bombings
Nowhere to go

Leaving children crying
On their own

Everyone needs it
Peace!

Jasmin Kogelbauer (10)
The Russell School, Richmond

A Football Pitch

A football pitch
It has goals
Dirty, long, wide
It is like a rectangle with lines
It is like a green sea of grass
It makes me feel happy
As happy as a person
Who has achieved their goal
A football pitch
It reminds me about
How we should enjoy life to the full.

Billy Butler (10)
Wildridings Primary School, Bracknell

The Hairy Spider

The hairy spider
Eight-legged creature
That makes its home wherever
Hairy, big, scary
Like a legged carpet
Catches its prey on its home
It makes me feel huge
The hairy spider
Reminds us how careless we are.

Jack Lindsey (10)
Wildridings Primary School, Bracknell

The Blue Monkey

The blue monkey
Who is one year old

Sad, small, friendly
Like a baby in my arms
Snuggled up like a charm

I feel like a sister to him
I'm the only one he trusts

The blue monkey
Ropes and leaves all around
But no monkeys to be seen.

Courtney Meers (10)
Wildridings Primary School, Bracknell

A Flamingo

A flamingo
Feathers from white to pink

Tall, skinny, fluffy
Like a ball of pink feathers
Like a balancing champ
They make me feel full of colour
Like a rainbow in the sky

A flamingo
They make me feel as free as a bird.

Alice Morgan (10)
Wildridings Primary School, Bracknell

The Red Rose

The red rose
It's a tall stem with thorns
Elegant, long, radiant
Like a love letter of red
Its thorns defend like swords
It fills me with passion
And makes me delicate
It makes me passionate as a poet
The red rose
To remind us to be peaceful and respect others.

Kenesha Barracliffe (11)
Wildridings Primary School, Bracknell

The Shooting Star

Shooting star
The star shoots over us
Shiny, bright and beautiful
As bright as the sun
As bright as the moon
It makes me feel amazing
As amazing as the star
The shooting star
It helps us remember
To keep the world a better place to live in.

Abigail Harris (10)
Wildridings Primary School, Bracknell

The Teacher

The teacher
Is there to help you learn
Stressy, knowledgeable, friendly
Like a normal person
Like a brain with two feet
They make me happy
Like they are in your family
The teacher
Reminds you that *you* should listen.

Helen Fish (10)
Wildridings Primary School, Bracknell

The Train

Built to be on rails
Speedy, powerful, mighty
Like a monster chasing you
Like a dragon in fury
It makes me feel slow
Like a snail that everyone passes
The train
Reminds us of how quickly time passes.

James Hemington (10)
Wildridings Primary School, Bracknell

The Shiny Mirror

The shiny mirror
Made thousands of years ago
Big, small, pretty
Like the shining sun
Like an image of you
It makes me feel like there's two of me
But one is better
It feels like everyone is double
The shiny mirror
Reminds you of a twin.

Yasmin Senussi (10)
Wildridings Primary School, Bracknell

Raven

Raven
The great raven
Mystical, magnificent, extraordinary
Like a kite flying in the breeze
Like a guard in the sky
It makes me feel scared
Like being chased by a *giant*
The great raven
Reminds me how big the world is.

Tyler Jones (10)
Wildridings Primary School, Bracknell

Young Writers Information

We hope you have enjoyed reading this book - and that you will continue to enjoy it in the coming years.

If you like reading and writing poetry drop us a line, or give us a call, and we'll send you a free information pack.

Alternatively if you would like to order further copies of this book or any of our other titles, then please give us a call or log onto our website at www.youngwriters.co.uk

**Young Writers Information
Remus House
Coltsfoot Drive
Peterborough
PE2 9JX**

(01733) 890066